THE SOCIAL USES OF WRITING

Politics and Pedagogy

Interpretive Perspectives on Education and Policy

George W. Noblit and William T. Pink, **Series Editors**

The Social Uses of Writing: Politics and Pedagogy, Thomas Fox

in preparation

Critical Role of Teachers in the Social Order, Barry Kanpol

Schools and Constructed Systems, Charles A. Tesconi

The Schools They Left Behind, Alan De Young

Staff Development for School Change, William T. Pink and Arthur A. Hyde (Eds.)

Testing, Reform, and Rebellion, H. Dickson Corbett and Bruce L. Wilson

THE SOCIAL USES OF WRITING

Politics and Pedagogy

Thomas Fox
California State University, Chico

 ABLEX PUBLISHING CORPORATION
NORWOOD, NEW JERSEY

Copyright © 1990 by Ablex Publishing Corporation

Printed in the United States of America.

Library of Congress Cataloging-in-Publication Data

Fox, Thomas.
    The social uses of writing : politics and pedagogy / Thomas Fox.
      p. cm.—(Interpretive perspectives on education and policy)
    Includes bibliographical references.
    ISBN 0-89391-601-3
    1. English language—Composition and exercises—Study and teaching—Political aspects. 2. English language—Composition and exercises—Study and teaching—Social aspects. 3. English language—Rhetoric—Study and teaching—Political aspects. 4. English language—Rhetoric—Study and teaching—Social aspects. I. Title. II. Series.
PE1404.F687   1990
808'.042'07—dc20   89-78106
                                                      CIP

Ablex Publishing Corporation
355 Chestnut Street
Norwood, New Jersey 07648

for Jean

Table of Contents

Series Preface   ix

Acknowledgments   xi

1 Seeing Students as People   1

      The Political Frame   5
      An Interactive Classroom   13
      Seeing Students as People   20

2 Seeing Teachers as People   25

      Teachers as Ethnographers   25
      The Goals of Ethnography   27
      Ethnography's Limits   29
      Problem-Posing Teachers   37
      The Problem with Posing Problems: History Revisited   42
      The Political Teacher   43
      Seeing Teachers as People   45

Introduction to the Case Studies   49

3 Gender Interests in Reading and Writing   51

      Beauty and "The Birth-Mark"   53
      Competition, Persuasion, and Masculinity   60

4 The Rhetoric of a Working-Class Student   71

5 Writing is Like an Enemy: Schooling and the Language
   of a Black Student   89

6 Teachers Don't Teach Alone   109

      Interpretation in Writing Courses   109
      Two Texts   111

Judgment   114
Interpreting the Classroom   115
Conflict at the Center   117
Teachers Don't Teach Alone   119

Appendix   123

Studying Social Groups and Literacy   123

References   127

Author Index   135

Subject Index   137

Series Preface
Interpretive Perspectives on Education and Policy

William T. Pink, *National College of Education, National–Louis University*

George W. Noblit, *University of North Carolina at Chapel Hill*

Historically, educational policy research has reflected the point of view of policy makers and as a consequence represents the interests of those in power. Their voices are loud and clear in the debates on what is and should be the nature of education and schools. Indeed, these voices have largely defined both the boundaries and the substance of these debates. The consequence is that educational policy research has developed as a language of control and compliance that conceptualizes students, educators, and citizens as obstacles to the realization of effective policy outcomes. The result is a litany of studies that shows how the implementation of (primarily top-down) policy has failed. Rather than rethinking the process and implementation of educational policy, policy makers resort to increased efforts at control, recreating the image of students, educators, and citizens as recalcitrant and resistent. The circularity of this reasoning has proved both reproductive and counter-productive to realizing meaningful change in schools. Policy makers increase their control while the people subjected to the policies increase their resistance. There is no way out of this circularity without (1) changing the language of educational policy, (2) developing greater sensitivity to the impact of context on implementation, and (3) expanding the boundaries and substance of the debate over policy.

Changing the language, the boundaries, and substance of the debate over educational policy will not be easy. Those in power correctly recognize the threat of this enterprise to the current conception and governance of schools. Moreover, there are few forums for new languages to be created and explored for their potential. This is the purpose of the series titled, *Interpretive Perspectives on Education and Policy.*

We believe that a new language can come from looking closely at education as people create it, giving voice to their purposes, understandings, and interests. These voices can easily be ignored, however, unless they are expressed in the wider discourse about education and policy. This series titled, *Interpretive Perspectives on Education and Policy,* is one way to privilege these voices. Each book in the series is based on a close study of the lived experiences of citizens, students, and/or educators, and articulates their interpretation of these experiences. The authors have the additional responsibility of representing these voices in the wider discourse about educational policy. In brief, the charge to authors has been to undertake a thorough analysis of some aspect of education, *and* to fully explore the implications of their findings for educational policy. We suggest that these interpretations and critiques provide essential insights about schooling from which we can develop the new perspectives on education and policy which are so urgently needed.

William T. Pink
George W. Noblit

Acknowledgments

I would like to thank the following people for their support: Jean Schuldberg, Nicky Fox, Louise Fox, Don and Roberta-Jean Fox, Irving and Jane Schuldberg, Anne Fox-Hayward, Marilyn Sternglass, Deborah Tannen, Judith Green, Deborah Brandt, and my editors William Pink and George Noblit. Thanks to the Department of English and the College of Humanities and Fine Arts at California State University, Chico (especially Don Heinz and Carol Burr) for giving me the time, working conditions, and good cheer so I could complete this book. Finally, special thanks to David Bleich for his encouragement, great conversation, and friendship.

1
Seeing Students as People

Readers of earlier versions of this study occasionally asked the question, "Are you trying to show how gender, class, and race affect reading and writing or are you arguing for a certain type of pedagogy?" And for these readers, the two aims were in conflict. I argued then, as I am arguing now, that given the present social conditions of our classrooms, these two aims are inseparable. Any argument about the nature of literacy in the classroom necessarily involves an argument about its origins in a pedagogy, and any argument for a particular writing/reading pedagogy assumes, or preferably defines, a particular conception of language. Both students' and teachers' language in the classroom grows from expectations of what is appropriate, and these expectations, in turn, are shaped by our past experiences in classrooms. Historically, classroom language has excluded the home or street language of many women, working-class, and minority students, discouraging students from presenting themselves as members of social groups. So when I ask my students, "what are the effects of your particular social history on your reading and writing styles in the classroom?", posing the question itself argues for what I call an "interactive" pedagogy, for without a pedagogy that will allow an answer to this question, the answer would be "no effect at all." Both the question and its answer require a changed classroom context. This changed context, in my view, would be one where students consciously examine the interplay of their social experience with their educational experience. Throughout this book, I refer to this double context: a social structure that stratifies people according to gender, class, and race and the classroom as it is understood by the students and myself.

This study, like others, has a multitude of origins. I could cite my family's concern with political issues, an undergraduate literature course that suggested the political potential of studying reading and writing, the Feminist Criticism group at Indiana University for helping me understand not only how gender affects language, but how status, privilege, and opportunity affect all discourse. One source that will be apparent to readers familiar with reader-response criticism is David Bleich's (1975, 1986, 1988) work. I was fortunate to begin my teaching experience with Bleich in 1981 when he invited me to teach as one of four assistants in an experimental course entitled "Studying One's Own Language." As the title suggests, Bleich

organized his course so that students could undertake a systematic exploration of their reading and writing habits. The lectures, discussions, essay
topics, and analytical assignments integrated developmental and life cycle
psychology with Bleich's characteristic focus on the shaping force of actual
important relationships in the language user's life history.[1] The students'
remarkable success in talking and writing about their language use, especially
in the retrospective summaries of their understanding of reading and writing
habits, revealed enthusiasm and sophistication well beyond what I had
previously considered freshman level.

Encouraged by this experience, two colleagues and I developed an approach
that applied many of these same concepts to a regular freshman writing
course.[2] Although the syllabus changed gradually, I consciously transformed
what was primarily a course that asked students to understand their language
use in light of a universal life cycle and a unique life history to one that
sees language use as a part of a social system that unequally distributes
privilege, status, and opportunity on the basis of, among other categories,
gender, class, and race. (See the Appendix for the general shape of this
course.)

The transformation of my teaching mirrored, and was influenced by, a
movement in writing theory and pedagogy away from the cognitive and
individualist sets of assumptions that initially fueled the process movement,
towards a social model of writing. Kenneth Bruffee's (1984) explorations
into the connections between conversation and writing and his interest in
peer tutoring resulted in a bibliographic article that sums up both the
promise and the problems with social models of writing, and marks the
acceptance of social theories of writing. "Social Construction, Language,
and the Authority of Knowledge: A Bibliographic Essay" (1986) capsulizes
the implications of social constructionist thought for writing teachers and
researchers. Bruffee defines social construction as follows:

> A social constructionist position in any discipline assumes that entities we
> normally call reality, knowledge, thought, facts, texts, selves, and so on are
> constructs generated by communities of like-minded peers. Social construction
> understands reality, knowledge, thought, facts, texts, selves, and so on as
> community-generated and community-maintained linguistic entities—or, more
> broadly speaking, symbolic entities—that define or "constitute" the commu-
> nities that generate them. . . . (p. 774)

---

[1] See David Bleich, *Readings and Feelings: An Introduction to Subjective Criticism* (1975),
Subjective Criticism (1978), and particularly, *The Double Perspective* (1988) for more information about the principles and practices of this course.

[2] This seems like a good opportunity to thank John Clower and Elisabeth Daeumer. They
collaborated in the development of this syllabus, contributed essay topics, and helped develop
some of the ideas for this study.

Bruffee, after citing Kuhn, Rorty, Geertz as his base, goes on to suggest the implications of social construction for composition:

> social constructionist work in composition is based on the assumption that writing is primarily a social act. A writer's language originates with a community to which he or she belongs. We use language primarily to join communities we do not yet belong to and to cement our membership in communities we already belong to. (p. 784)

Social theories of knowledge and language had much to do with my aim of exploring how students' social backgrounds affected their language in the writing classroom. And Bruffee (and others, most notably, David Bartholomae [1985] and Patricia Bizzell [1982, 1986a, 1986b]), did much to instigate social approaches to studying and learning writing.

Although social constructionist thought seems to represent a politically promising departure from individualist philosophy, in the actual practice of the everyday writing classroom the change may only be theoretical. We can see the problems with the moderate version of social constructionist thought in Bruffee's (1984) practice-oriented article, "Peer Tutoring and the 'Conversation of Mankind'." Bruffee states that peer tutoring—and, by implication, education in general—asks students to "loosen ties with the knowledge community they currently belong to and join another" (p. 12). Such a view contradicts a more liberating pedagogy, for Bruffee assumes that the academic community is unchangeably separate and apparently superior to students' knowledge community. Such a view only serves to continue the exclusion of home and street language and culture from education, continuing the separation of specific social identity and learning.

This moderate version of social construction shows up in Bruffee's citations of sources, and signals the general reluctance of writing teachers and researchers to embrace politics. Bruffee most heavily relies on philosophers and literary critics who stress "social" over "political," such as Richard Rorty (1979) or Stanley Fish (1980). He completely ignores feminism's contribution to social constructionist thought (see Marilyn Frye's *The Politics of Reality: Essays on Feminist Theory* [1983], many of the essays in Sandra Harding and Merrill B. Hintikka's *Discovery Reality* [1983], and Dale Spender's introduction to *Men's Studies Modified* [1981]). Finally, although Marxism has been central to the formulation of social construction, very few Marxists are cited in Bruffee's article, and when they are cited, the political content of their work is absent. Bruffee does not deal with the following implications of social construction: multiple versions of knowledge and reality exist, some versions of knowledge and reality are in conflict, and some communities' versions of knowledge and reality are privileged over others.[3]

Patricia Bizzell (1986a) discusses Kuhn, Rorty, and Fish and acknowledges the essentially social character of language and knowledge in "Foundationalism and Anti-Foundationalism in Composition Studies." Unlike Bruffee, however, she acknowledges the essentially political implications of such thought by not only discussing how student writing is socially constructed, but by emphasizing that academic writing is also socially constructed. Her emphasis leads her to a more critical understanding of the academic community. Bizzell concludes, like Bruffee, that

> because we believe that the discourse constitutes the knowledge, we can argue that beginning one's initiation into the discipline with some acquaintance with its knowledge is a good route to familiarity with its discourse conventions and assumptions. (p. 53)

However, Bizzell more complexly embraces the contradictions of such a conclusion. She asks:

> But what provision can we find in this pedagogy for the students whose initial contact with academic discourse seems to present no choices other than deracination from a home discourse community or expulsion from the academic community? (p. 53)

This question, posed specifically for working-class, black, and women students, motivates my research as much as any other. And her answer is congruent with the stance I take in this work: "Scholars must simply acknowledge political activity as a professional responsibility" (p. 53).

Up until my experience teaching with Bleich, I had been teaching and learning in fairly conventional classrooms, ones where issues of politics and responsibility seemed absent. I progressed through graduate school with the nagging feeling that my life—experiences, values, convictions—was growing more and more separate from my career in English. My family, parents and siblings both, had always stressed the importance and responsibility of enacting one's political values in everyday life. As I graduated from lower-division to upper-division to graduate English courses, then from taking courses to teaching them, these values seemed to be excluded more and more. The move to reverse this trend, to try to unite my teaching practices

---

[3] For a complementary critique, see Greg Myers (1986). Myers argues that Bruffee uncritically accepts reality as it is socially constructed: "But while Bruffee shows that reality can be seen as a social construct, he does not give us any way to criticize this construct. Having discovered the role of consensus in the production of knowledge, he takes this consensus as something that just is, rather than something that might be good or bad" (p. 166).

with the values of my background, parallels the task that I ask of my students. I, too, had to confront my educational history and examine my classroom language.

Formulating and teaching this approach and the subsequent exploration of it in this study enact two general political convictions: promoting a tolerant understanding of socially diverse people, and working to enlarge the world of those groups to whom our social structure has denied privilege, opportunity, and status. As such I hope to acknowledge, as Bizzell suggests we must, political activity as a professional responsibility.

THE POLITICAL FRAME

Although the approach and this study evolved to reflect a more direct relationship between politics and language use, I retained a number of features of Bleich's approach that I will discuss in the following chapters, among them, a continuing focus on face-to-face encounters (including the one between student and teacher), the use of small groups, analytical papers asking students to understand each others' language use, and a final retrospective analysis. Issues related to developmental psychology do not disappear when the subject matter changes from "adolescence" and "important relationships" to memberships in social groups. Students can connect an important relationship with a parent, for instance, to the way that they were socialized as men and women, or show how a parent's insecurity about social location was transformed into a desire for upward mobility, or show how racial identity motivates adolescent slang. I sought to retain the feelings of enthusiasm that I saw in Bleich's students, enthusiasm growing from integrating language study with actual face-to-face encounters. However, I asked my students to understand these encounters within a social and political frame.

Students reported and analyzed actual experiences with language centered around essay topics related to the categories of gender, class, and race. These categories functioned as *interpretive frames*. The sense with which I use this phrase differs slightly from the sense of background knowledge or a set of expectations based on past experience. Certainly, in asking students to consider their experiences in understanding language use I quite consciously asked them to draw on their background knowledge. But in most research, the use of the term *interpretive frame* refers to assumptions that are *unconsciously* or *habitually* drawn upon by speakers or interpreters. In the case of the political interpretive frame in this study, the frame was imposed by the teacher, placed from above, so to speak, in a context where students did not expect to use it. I intended this frame to focus the topics students could choose to write about in their personal essays, shape class and small group discussions, and provide a set of questions and possible interpretations for students to explore in their analytical papers and final retrospective essays.

The interpretive frames of gender, class, and race ask students to understand their language in explicitly political terms. For whatever other associations one may have to these social categories, they have been historically allied with important social issues and political movements. Along these social divisions, our social structure most obviously and unequally distributes social and economic privileges, status, and opportunities. Not many students (or anyone else) doubt that discrimination occurs against women or that blacks suffer from prejudice, or that working-class people have less opportunity than wealthy people. There is, of course, a great deal of disagreement among students on the degree of discrimination, the cause, who is responsible for it, and what to do about it. But no one doubts the legitimacy of the categories. Long histories of political movements, Seneca Falls, abolition, the periodic workers' movements that have attended the growth of industrial society, as well as contemporary feminism, civil rights, and Marxism, prove the durability of these categories in explaining social life.[4]

The use of these categories has two explicit political aims. The first is to promote tolerance of diverse styles of communication, showing that all instances of language use can make sense provided the interpreter has the knowledge with which to understand. In this, I wish to replicate in my classroom, on an immediate, face-to-face level, the kind of effect that William Labov's "The Logic of Non-Standard English" (1972) had on the understanding of black English. Labov's work exploded the view that urban black speakers used language illogically or deficiently. The second consequence I hope to accomplish is more ambitious. If students learn to articulate how and why they read and write as they do, if they explain this "how" and "why" in terms of gender, class, and race, then this knowledge can be put to use in altering those aspects of language use that students feel work against their interests. The consciousness of the how and why, in ideal cases, has political consequences. I phrase this tentatively because the claim that an experience in an introductory writing course can have certain political consequences is a difficult one to make. One objection is that such consequences are difficult to see, given the fact that all students write for the teacher. How would one distinguish between a political realization and compliance with the teacher? Even if one seemed to really change consciousness, there is no guarantee that

---

[4] These three categories do not, of course, exhaust the important social divisions in our culture: sexual orientation, religious affiliation, and age come to mind as other important social categories.

consciousness leads to active or positive change. Students may realize the ways in which their language reproduces social stratifications that work to their disadvantage yet feel powerless to change, or students may realize how their language supports their own social advantage and be unwilling to change. In my discussions of student work in Chapters Three through Five, I have included examples that show varied degrees of political awareness and willingness or ability to make related changes. Ms. M (Chapter Three) and Mr. C (Chapter Four) both show a significant change in the way they understand language use and both indicate a potential to alter the way they use and understand language. Ms. N (Chapter Five) began with a politically complex understanding of language use, yet all along she understandably felt powerless to effect any change. Mr. H (Chapter Three), on the other hand, saw his language use as reproducing masculine ideology, and seemed uninterested in altering it. I am encouraged enough by experiences with students like Mr. C and Ms. M to feel that language study of the type I present in this book does, at times, have the political consequence I intend.

Students certainly don't expect political consequences to issue from freshman English. What they do expect is based on their educational experience, especially in English classes. These expectations include conceptions of how to present themselves in the classroom, and how not to present themselves. Although students know their social identity, they aren't prepared to *be* this identity in the classroom. For many students, particularly minorities, women, and working-class students, to present themselves primarily in terms of these social identities would be to risk incurring the social prejudices against these social groups. For middle-class students, white students, and men, these social identities represent the norm and as such, there is not much motivation to claim them. Students learn through educational experience to exclude their social background as a resource for learning and understanding. In the case of discriminated groups, students come to see this background as a liability and a barrier to success in the classroom.

Students instead learn to leave their social identity outside the classroom and behave within the confines of two concepts, Student and Individual, or better, a combination, Individual Student. As Students, they expect to be given and follow directions on how to pass the course or get an "A," show eagerness and motivation, neither of which may overtly stem from practical or social experience, but must come from a more Student-like source, the suitably abstract "desire to learn" or "thirst for knowledge." As Individuals, they expect to be judged according to a single standard of ability, and hope to be found unique, unusual, or best yet, exceptional. These generalizations of students' experiences don't apply in an absolute way to all students, for surely some students have had exceptional teachers and exceptional schools. For others, their experience may be even worse than I've suggested. I will help to give some substance and actuality to these generalizations by examining student writing and briefly look at conceptions of writers and readers by other scholars.

The following comments by students of mine in analytical papers illustrate the type of expectations students bring to English courses:

> When I started this class, it seemed ridiculous to examine my writing for specific influences such as gender, ethnicity and social class. I felt as though none of these areas would factor into what I wrote.

> Before enrolling in this class, I believed that when a person writes, he wrote what happened to pop into his head. The ideas of taking a stance, writing in terms of masculinity, relationships affecting writing . . . seemed ludicrous.

In these passages, both students shape their learning experience for my benefit. Both go on, afterwards, to testify to the value of looking at writing in terms of social identity. In all honesty, one needs to read such accounts with some degree of skepticism. There's an outside chance that my ideas *remained* ludicrous and ridiculous. No matter, my point remains: Students do not expect freshman English to involve anything remotely like "taking a stance." These statements, by default, indicate what these two students did expect: uncommitted writing, writing which was divorced from experience related to gender, class, and race, and individualistic writing. In turn, this type of writing suggests the kind of person they anticipated being in my classroom.

One can see similar attitudes in the essays students wrote on the first day of class. I ask my students, after explaining the course policies, to "write an essay telling the class who you are." These essays support my contention that students expect to be understood only as Students and Individuals. Naturally all of these essays differ, but they usually include two common features. The first is that at some point in the essay, students will talk about the subject matter of writing. These statements help establish their identities as Students in the teacher's eyes. Here are a few representative examples:

> I like to be optimistic and feel if you don't believe in yourself, no one else will.

> Although I love to have fun, it doesn't mean neglect of my education or my body. I am very serious about both.

> Right now, I've realized that writing is an essential skill that I have to know!

> This incident demonstrates the necessity of clear thinking and writing.

The other standard feature is the inclusion of information that differentiates students as individuals. Frequently, students will cite hobbies, talents, or experiences that they consider to be unique or memorable, such as their expertise in rock climbing or a recent trip to Europe. This information functions in the student-teacher relationship to establish a unique, individualized identity along with the student role. Although some students say, "I am Irish" or "I am ¾ Slovenian," most students seem to avoid such descriptions. I have never had a student present his or her experience as a function of one of the three social categories.[5]

That students don't present themselves as political or social beings in the classroom is certainly understandable; their educational experience inhibits it. Richard Ohmann (1976) has shown, in *English in America,* how the exclusion of students' social identity is a part of the historical exclusion of political topics in both literature and composition instruction. Particularly germane to this study is Ohmann's survey of composition textbooks. Composition textbooks are probably the best example Ohmann could study, for they are the most widely used type of text in English, they are written for the student, and they are surely influential in circumscribing the possible roles for students. Ohmann surveyed 14 composition textbooks—"rhetorics", not theory books—to see what assumptions these texts make about student writing and writers. Ohmann's observations support my understanding that students learn to conceive of themselves abstractly as Students:

> "The" student—intended audience of all but one of the books—is defined only by studenthood, not by any other attributes. (p. 145)

> For in abstracting "the student" away from society and history, and in treating composition as an activity apart from politics, the textbooks very narrowly fix the student's imagined circumstances and the possibilities for action there. (p. 147)

In conceiving of themselves as abstractions, students consequently limit the goals and achievements that they consider possible or appropriate in the English classroom. The following quotation from one of my students, written at the end of my course, illustrates this limitation. The fact that I used no textbook and taught a course designed to work against these limitations demonstrates the generality of the role of the student as defined by "Studenthood" and show what a powerful ideology it is:

I am a student in this class with a goal to successfully complete this course

---

[5] See Chapter Four for a further discussion of this essay topic. The student whose work I discuss in that chapter provides an excellent example of a student who presents himself as both an abstraction (a Student) and a unique individual.

and my fellow students are striving for the same thing. It is this idea which helps us with our writing. We all know we are in the same position and we will do whatever it takes to make it a success.

The "same position" that this student speaks of is "Studenthood" and the consequent definition of success (need it be said?) is a good grade. The idea of studenthood that Ohmann discovered, in addition to limiting the students' conception of themselves, divided students from their social backgrounds:

> He is classless, sexless though generically male, timeless. (p. 145)

> [The textbooks] see him as newborn, unformed, without social origins and without needs that would spring from his origins. He has no history. (p. 148)

Finally, these textbooks see him (for "he" is generically male) in isolation, as an individual:

> One more thing: the student is almost invariably conceived of as an individual. He acts not only out of time and history, but *alone*. . . . (p. 149)

Ohmann's analysis of textbooks indicates the way professional textbook writers conceive of the student writer, and gives an indication of the way teachers and students themselves understand the writer. I see the same sort of pattern in the way reader-response critics understand "the reader." I take as my primary examples two reader-response critics who have also been interested in applying their theories of reading to teaching, Norman Holland (1975) and Steven Mailloux (1982). These two theorists represent what I see as the two common ways of understanding readers: as individuals or as abstractions.[6]

Norman Holland takes individual diversity, what Jonathan Culler (1981) calls "the individuality of the individual" (p. 53), as the issue to which he directs his study, *5 Readers Reading*. Holland tested and interviewed college-age students to determine how their "identity themes" influence their inter-

---

[6] Other reader critics who see readers as individuals are Walter Slatoff, *With Respect to Readers: Dimensions of Literary Response* (1970), and Eugene R. Kintgen, *The Perception of Poetry* (1982). Although David Bleich's work is often linked with Holland's and with an individually-oriented approach, he differs significantly from Holland in that Bleich always understands his individual readers in terms of their relationships with others, including the teacher and the researcher. Critics who see readers as abstractions include Stanley Fish, *Is There a Text in This Class?* (1980), Wolfgang Iser, *The Act of Reading* (1978), and Jonathan Culler, *Structuralist Poetics* (1975). Three reader critics stand out as exceptions: Louise Rosenblatt, *Literature as Exploration*, (1983), Judith Fetterly, *The Resisting Reader* (1978), and Elizabeth A. Flynn, "Gender and Reading" (1983a). Note that the three exceptions are women critics. Flynn also notes that women reader-response critics commonly do see reading in a social context; see Elizabeth A. Flynn, "Women as Reader-Response Critics" (1983b).

pretation of literature. Identity themes are something like a person's core personality, described by Holland as the constant theme upon which one "lives out variations, much as a musician can infinitely vary a single musical motif to create a theme and variations" (p. 56). Holland sees these identity themes as unchangeable, an *underlying* reality upon which all social, ethical, or political understandings are superimposed. By asserting the reality of these identity themes, he prevents understanding readers as social beings.

Consider his analysis of the radical reader, Shep, the most politically minded of the five readers. Perhaps because Holland's research did not take place in the classroom, or perhaps because it took place in the more politically active 1960s, Shep was more overtly political than most students. He consistently saw the issues of the stories as enmeshed in a sociocultural milieu, frequently involving relations between blacks and whites, rich and poor, the powerful and the powerless. A good example of Shep's view is his understanding of the role of Judy Jones, in Fitzgerald's "Winter Dreams," a story he says treats people as property or things: " 'She's something you can get if you've got next year's model. She's next year's model, too. You get 'em both at the same time. And I think that's obscene' " (p. 341). But Holland transforms this social and political indictment of fetishism and sexism in "Winter Dreams" into a short discussion of "body products":

> Shep's imagining Judy as a high-priced car derives from a child's fantasies about his body products. Are they a part of him and alive or are they separate and dead? Are they precious and high-priced or are they disgusting wastes? (p. 342)

Holland's analyses consistently place a social and political interpretation in a secondary, marginal relationship to his understanding of psychoanalysis. He clearly states the irrelevance of readers' social experience:

> Nothing in this study will support that idea or suggest that superficial resemblances of gender, age, culture or class (in a Marxist sense, for example) have any important role in and of themselves in response. What counts are the deeper structures of adaptation of lifestyle. (p. 205)

Readers, like Shep, sometimes do see gender, age, culture, and class (in the Marxist sense) as important aspects of response. But in Holland's research, socially-based responses are considered "superficial," to be transformed by the critic into "deeper" discussions of individual identities.

Holland's claim that readers are free from social influences seems most fragile when he discusses the "maidenly" Sandra, the only woman reader out of the five, and claims that "Sandra's identity theme seemed the same kind of statement as the male readers" (p. 101), disparaging any attempt to insist that gender is an important factor. And yet Sandra's identity theme, which Holland summarizes as: *"to see and approach more and more closely a source of power and nurture, but not to see its loss"* (p. 103), and her recurrent wish, according to Holland, to equalize "a flow of power from stronger to weaker" (p. 103), seems absolutely inseparable not only from her place in society as a woman, but her place in a research situation with a male "full professor in what one might call the prime of life" (p. 62). We can see in Holland's explications of Shep and Sandra how obviously social and political understandings of readers can be shaped by the power of the researcher, critic, or teacher into isolated individuals. Like the composition textbooks that prevent students from seeing shared political interests by defining students as isolated from each other, teachers who take Holland's model of the reader prevent students from seeing how shared social experiences produce interpretations.[7]

Most reader-response critics don't consider the work of actual readers, as Holland does. Usually, reader-response critics rely on some version of a hypothetical reader, such as the "informed reader," the "competent reader," or the "implied reader."[8] These hypothetical readers serve as models for what readers *would* do. Yet the hypothetical reader may as effectively serve to exclude conscious attention to politics from reading as Holland's individualism. In fact, most of these models combine the individualism of Holland with the abstractions that Ohmann cited in the composition textbooks. David Bleich (1986) recently made this point:

> models [of readers] presuppose the idea of a single person facing a single text as a reasonable or even natural way of including the subjectivity of reading in the study of literature. But as this presupposition is variously used, the "reader" has become more and more a purely hypothetical being. (p. 402)

Susan Suleiman (1980), in her introduction to *The Reader in the Text*, makes a similar point, specifically in regard to Iser's use of the "implied reader:"

> Given that [Iser's approach] promises to take account of the experience of the individual subject, it is important to note that the individual subject is often indistinguishable from an abstract and generalized "reader." (p. 26)

This individualized abstraction excludes a conception of a reader with a

---

[7] Holland's (1977) pedagogical essays seem to be closer to the point of view that I advocate. In "Transactive Teaching: Cordelia's Death" he claims that his style of teaching is a means of understanding "one's transactions of social and political realities" (p. 277). But Holland's understanding of identity in *5 Readers Reading* (1975) would prevent this possibility.

[8] The hypothetical readers of Fish (1980), Culler (1975), and Iser (1978), respectively.

distinct and important social background. Reader-response critics often justify their exclusion of political issues by appealing to the primacy of this hypothetical reader over the real reader who inhabits the social world. Steven Mailloux (1982), in defending his use of "the implied reader" in his reading of "Rappacini's Daughter" in *Interpretive Conventions: The Reader in American Fiction,* claims that his account of the reader's activity is "descriptive." Furthermore, a "descriptive" account is free from the influence of a social group memberships. Mailloux acknowledges, for instance, feminist readings, but asserts that a description of the "implied reader's" response is prior to (and implicitly superior to) such a reading:

> Only after a reader-response description is completed or assumed can a feminist critique begin. The (explicit or assumed) *description* cannot be antifeminist; only the further use (or non-use) of it can be. (p. 89n)

Although Mailloux's approach is philosophically different than Holland's, the result is the same. Both critics propose a structure of the reader that is individual, unchangeable, and prior to the responses of readers in the social world. Both critics argue for the precedence of their conception of the reader over a social reader. Either method effectively banishes political concerns from entering into ideas about reading.

These descriptions of how writers and readers are individualized and abstracted reflect a widespread set of conceptions about who students are or should be in the English classroom. Composition textbooks and reader-response critics did not suddenly impose this identity on the student. Instead, these examples illustrate general habits of teachers and students alike, ones which are built up in day-to-day experiences in classrooms.[9]

AN INTERACTIVE CLASSROOM

Any activist pedagogy has to confront the power of history. To do so is to begin with the students' educational history, their well-rehearsed habit of suppressing social aspects of their identity, and the self-imposed limitations that accompany this habit. What happens when these students confront a teacher who asks them to examine their language in terms of gender, class, and race? The political frame represents a sure challenge to students' expectations of an English course. I set it up clearly and without ambiguity: Students in their analytical papers were to show how

---

[9] Examples of research that explores how individualized and abstracted conceptions of students serve the interests of a stratified society include: Richard Ohmann, *English in America* (1976), and Richard Sennett and Jonathan Cobb, *The Hidden Injuries of Class* (1973) (socioeconomic class); Dale Spender, *Invisible Women: The Schooling Scandal* (1982) (gender); John U. Ogbu, *Minority Education and Caste* (1978) (race).

gender, class, and race affected their language use. I lectured on gender and language, class and language, and ethnicity and language.[10] I passed out a course schedule with these same topics as subheadings. And yet, students entered my course with influential experiences that had led them to exclude, by habit or by will, these very issues.

All of the written work by students presented in this study should be understood, in part, as the students' negotiation between a powerful history of excluding discussion of social identity and the necessity to include it in my course—as the *interaction* of the political frame (the imposed context) and classroom contexts. This interaction is extremely complex. As I have said, students usually construct the teacher as someone who encourages the exclusion of social identity. Yet the political frame asks for exactly this information. Students are wisely skeptical of my course, and frequently wonder if I hold a secret agenda, one that looks more like the English courses they are used to. This skepticism often involves an interaction where the student takes small risks, as Ms. N did (Chapter Five), to test the teacher's sincerity, to see if what appears to be a course where the purpose is to understanding language use in terms of social categories, really is. We can understand this conflict between students' "historical" teacher and my stated goals as an internal one between how they have achieved success in the past, by excluding social information, and my unequivocal demand that they focus on this information in my course. One factor works in my favor; many students actually wish to explore and express the consequences of their social backgrounds. In cases where students feel discriminated against because of their background, they harbor a great deal of resentment at having to suppress it. Some students experience a great sense of relief; they feel encouraged and empowered to explore their social background, as in the case of Mr. C (Chapter Four). If students are trusting enough of my good intentions, or are tired enough of having to suppress their backgrounds, this wish to express themselves in terms of their social identity can combine with the wish to comply with the teacher and overcome their historically-based reluctance.

Although I have presented the conflict between the political frame and the student's history as a standard one (I do believe that all of my students experience some version of this conflict), students experience it in different ways, as the case studies in Chapters Three through Five attest. Each student perceives the problem of the political frame differently and each student's writing demonstrates the varying ways that students deal with this problem. One way of looking at their writing that is *not* possible,

---

[10] For a further discussion of these teaching practices, especially as they relate to the teacher's authority, see Chapter Two.

given the way I've conducted this study, is to see their writing and reading outside of the context of the interaction between student and teacher, outside the context of the history of excluding social identity and politics, and outside the political frame of my course.

The focus on context in studying language use has become commonplace in recent years. Speech act theory, especially, has been responsible for the focus; J. L. Austin (1962), John Searle (1969), and H. P. Grice (1975) turned their attention away from formal language features as responsible for carrying meaning to an exploration of the utterance in context. To understand language, in Austin's words, is to understand "the issuing of an utterance in a speech situation" (p. 138). Speech act theory understands "meaning" as "intention" and posits that the realization of the intention depends on its utterance in context. If a statement is uttered under the wrong circumstances, in the wrong context, then the utterance is, in Austin's words, "infelicitous" (pp. 13–19). Both "felicitous" and "infelicitous" statements are spoken in a context, but "infelicitous" statements "misfire" or constitute "abuses." Austin then goes on to state the qualities of language and context that must go together to make statements "felicitous": They must be uttered according to established conventions, by the appropriate person to the appropriate person, at the appropriate moment, and so on (pp. 14–15).

Austin's work, and those of his followers, has been beneficial in turning linguistics away from abstract and individualistic models, such as Chomsky's generative grammar, toward understanding language in a social context. Many speech act theorists, influenced by Austin's work, have attempted to map out detailed descriptions and lists of "appropriateness conditions," which attempt to pin down the contextual conditions necessary for language to make sense. But the listing aspect of speech act theory works against the understanding of language in *actual* contexts, and towards regularizing and formalizing an understanding of language use. Jacques Derrida (1977) bases his critique of Austin in "Signature Event Context" on this view of context; he asks, "are the conditions . . . of a context ever absolutely determinable?" (p. 174). His conclusion argues against such a determination:

> Every sign, linguistic or non-linguistic, spoken or written (in the current sense of this opposition), in a small or large unit, can be *cited,* put between quotation marks; in so doing it can break with every given context, engendering an infinity of new contexts in a manner which is absolutely illimitable. This does not imply that the mark is valid outside of a context, but on the contrary that there are only contexts without any center or absolute anchoring. (pp. 185–86)

There are some troubling aspects of Derrida's formulation, primarily, the absence of human agency (not even a decentered one), giving the impression that signs "cite" themselves and engender their own illimitable contexts. The other troubling aspect of this passage is the use of the term "citation." Its use in this passage implies that there could be such a thing as an "uncited" sign. But Derrida immediately states that "citation" is a characteristic "without which a mark could not even have a function called 'normal' " (p. 186). Citation, then, means that every sign functions in a special case, in a special context that is not self-evident or objective, as if every word had quotation marks around it. Derrida's essay contributes to a more complex understanding of context; context is no less the product of interpretation than sign.

The fact that contexts are "illimitable" does not reduce their necessity in explaining language. Instead, context needs to be revised from a self-evident, objective, and stable concept to one that is the product of interpretation and interaction. Contexts, then, do not precede language, but are in part created by it. Though powerfully shaped by their historical expectations, speakers' and listeners' creation of context need not remain stable among individuals or across time. Although I have already indicated that students' interpretation of the classroom context is not freely chosen, but influenced by the student's history, it does not follow that students, even with their shared histories, will necessarily interpret the context in the same way. Students construct and revise the classroom context through the continual interaction of teacher and student.

Students and teachers conduct this continual interaction, for the most part, in language. Note the difference between speech act theory and this view: Instead of context creating the conditions for understanding language, language—seen as interaction between two active participants—creates context. Meaning, then, does not result automatically when the appropriate utterance is spoken in the appropriate context, but results from a mutual negotiation of what is "appropriate." For instance, some students in my course never trust that the political frame of my course is an important part of the classroom context. These students continue to write the assignments, working diligently on perfecting academic prose, always believing that the real context of the classroom is similar to their experience in other English classrooms. The problem in cases like these is not that either party utters "infelicitous" statements, but that the student and the teacher did not establish—through linguistic interaction—a shared context.

What are the means by which student and teacher, in their interaction, create a context? Where the political context of gender, class, and race is an unexpected imposition, persuading the student to accept this conception of context becomes especially problematic. Students are sensitive to whether or not they share the teacher's conception of the context, whether or not they "get it." Because an interactive classroom makes demands that differ

from students' expectations, students frequently check or test their interpretation of the context; for instance, one student began his first analytical
paper with the following statement:

> First things first, I would like to state some of my personal feelings. Usually,
> I would not write this in a paper of this type, but I have learned to be more
> open in my writing in this class. I felt that this was a very difficult assignment.
> I have never analyzed anyone's language in this way and I don't know if I
> was accurate or not.

Despite this student's uncertainty as to how he completed the assignment,
I interpreted these comments to mean that the student most likely did share
my context. John J. Gumperz (1982), in *Discourse Strategies,* describes the
process of establishing and maintaining a shared context as the interpretation
of contextualization cues, which he defines as "any feature of linguistic
form that contributes to the signalling of contextual presuppositions" (p.
131). So when this student wrote, "I have never analyzed anyone's language
in this way," aside from the obvious information in this statement, I
interpreted it as a "contextualization cue" indicating that he has caught on
to the fact that I am presenting a learning context that differs from the
ones he has experienced in the past. When I responded to his cue of
uncertainty with comments and questions that engaged the issues he had
brought up in the paper, I signaled back to him (indirectly) that he had
understood the context as I had wished and that he should proceed with
this understanding.

We can also perceive when a shared context is not being built up.
Sometimes, because these cues are indirectly signaled and perceived, teachers
and students are unaware of miscommunication on the basis of differing
understandings of context until an assignment that demands a shared context
is given. Thus, when a student, given an analytical assignment to discuss
the relationship between gender and writing, discusses organization and
errors (not an uncommon occurrence), I realize that together we had not
established the context that will achieve the goals I set for the course. I
signal this miscommunication of context by reasserting the political frame
in the form of questions and comments on the paper and by representing
the work that the student did achieve (even if on organization and errors)
in terms of the social group under discussion.

I define context in this study as the product of the interaction of the
teacher and the student. The special circumstances of the imposition of the
political frame complicates the usual classroom context. We can understand
this complication as the interplay of two contexts: (a) students' experience
in a society stratified on the basis of social groups, and (b) the classroom

as it was experienced by my students. In Chapters Three through Five, I call this a "double context."

These two contexts differ radically from each other. The one, the classroom as I and my students construct it, is an event, an actual occurrence. In this sense it is what one most commonly thinks of as context: a set of describable circumstances that affect an event—in the case of my classroom, a physical location, a temporal location, a set of requirements, and other conditions of the classroom. The other context, a society stratified along the social categories of gender, class, and race, is not a context in the sense that it is an event in a physical and temporal location. And yet, if we define context as the set of assumptions we build in order to make meaning, as in the sense of the helpful explainer saying, "let me put it in context for you," then gender, class, and race count as contextual elements.

Given that I've defined context as interactionally established, is the context of the social categories interactionally established in the same way as the classroom context? Gumperz (1971), drawing upon Garfinkel's (1967) work in ethnomethodology, states: "Just as the meaning of words is always affected by context, social categories must be interpreted in terms of situational constraints" (p. 224). This point is crucial, for to understand the demand to explore social experience and language use in the classroom, one must understand the "situational constraints" of the classroom on the presentation of social experience. Social categories, in this volume, are not defined as sociological facts so much as by students' own interpretation and use of them. Working class, in Mr. C's instance (Chapter Four), is not a matter of absolute income, but the experience of what it means for him to see himself as "back in the pack" economically and socially. Students frequently will *not* disclose their social group membership because of their construction of the "situational constraints" of the classroom. One should not conclude, in such a case, that social experience is irrelevant; instead one needs to understand the social bases of the student's refusal to explore it (again, Mr. C's refusal in Chapter Four provides a good example).

Constraints have become a problematic term in recent literary theory. On one hand, context does limit or constrain the range of possible interpretations. But, on the other hand, crucial to any pedagogical theory is the fact that context also enables, makes new interpretations possible. For instance, my students did not naturally and spontaneously write about the influence of their social backgrounds on their language use; in fact, for most students, it seemed *unnatural* and forced. This fact does not reveal a lack of importance in the subject matter so much as the more historical regularity that, by habit or design, presenting social group membership has a negative effect on educational performance. Those who did, did so because of the inter-actionally constructed context that made possible their doing so.

Connecting these two understandings of context, individual events with the larger social structure is a task with which the ethnographer Clifford Geertz has been concerned. Geertz (1973) states, in *The Interpretation of Cultures,* that the task of the ethnographer is to produce "thick description" of individual events in order to understand how a culture works. Thick description, according to Geertz, is a "qualitative, highly participative and almost obsessively fine-comb field study in confined contexts" (p. 23), the aim of which is to trace "the curve of a social discourse; fixing it into an inspectable form" (p. 19). Geertz's attention to "events," to everyday occurrences in the actual lives of people in a culture, may not seem to some to be social analysis at all, but irrelevant accounts of idiosyncratic and unimportant behaviors, accounts of individual people or individual facts. Geertz has two answers to this charge. First he notes that culture exists and is reproduced in these small moments: "Culture exists in the trading post, the hill fort, or the sheep run" (p. 16); thus to study these events *is* to study culture. The second point Geertz makes is that ethnographies are what give "sensible actuality" (p. 23) to larger issues that social sciences are interested in; in his words, "small facts speak to large issues" (p. 23).

Understanding "small facts" of student behavior in terms of large social divisions is particularly difficult in the writing classroom, given the historical practice of excluding the political and the social. Teachers and students both need to interpret against the grain of tradition and the habits of Individualism and Studenthood. Students facing the political frame *have* to see their language socially and politically, just as teachers must assume a priori the political and social nature of language use. Such assumptions, because they are against habit, seem like "biases." But this assumes that the habits of individualism are unbiased or apolitical. Roger Simon and Donald Dippo (1986), in their summary article "On Critical Ethnographic Work," describe this approach:

> We view all modes of knowing and all particular knowledge forms as ideological, hence the issue is not whether one is "biased"; but rather, whose interests are served by one's work. (p. 196)

Simon and Dippo see all "descriptions" as organized by either an acknowledged or an unacknowledged problematic, "a particular structure of concepts which makes it possible to pose some kinds of questions while simultaneously suppressing the possibility of posing others" (p. 197). The stratification of our society along gender, class, and racial lines serves as the governing problematic that informs the analysis of student language and classroom contexts in the chapters that follow.

My interest in connecting the immediate events of the classroom context with the problematic of these abstract divisions of culture has to be a political one: I am arguing for seeing classroom events, the everyday events in actual classrooms that teachers and students regularly experience, as part of these larger social divisions, and the reverse as well, for these social divisions are a part of the everyday experience of the classroom.

SEEING STUDENTS AS PEOPLE

Once we see our students as members of a culture, once we see everyday student writing as a cultural event, then it is difficult to see student writing as produced by abstract and isolated Individual Students. Who wants to, anyway? An interactive classroom, based on the principles I've outlined in this chapter, has the following advantages.

Interaction demands that we see students as people, with experiences, with backgrounds, with linguistic resources. By demanding and expecting that this background be a part of the learning process, an interactive approach seeks to repair the damage done by educational practices that divide students from their backgrounds. For social experience to play a central role in writing classrooms, writing teachers need to conceive of the relationship between social backgrounds and students' classroom behavior. Crucial to the concept of interaction is to conceive of students as *agents,* not only actively constructing context, but also actively constructing, exploiting, concealing, resisting their backgrounds. Recent discussions of the politics of education have stressed the concept of "resistance," underlining the active nature of student participation in school. Henry Giroux (1981, 1983), in a number of books and articles, has been particularly articulate on this subject. Giroux seeks to revise what has been the dominant political interpretation of schooling and social class, the reproduction theory. This theory, best represented by Bourdieu and Passeron's *Reproduction in Education, Society, and Culture* (1977) and Bowles and Gintis' *Schooling in Capitalist America* (1976), demonstrates that schools reproduce inequalities of gender, class, and race through means of a "hidden curriculum" that socializes acceptance of existing social relationships, and through a formal curriculum that obscures or omits the experiences of working class students, women, and minorities. While acknowledging the value of such work, Giroux criticizes reproduction theories for being overly deterministic and pessimistic:

> [Reproductive] accounts often leave us with a view of schooling and domination that appears to have been pressed out of an Orwellian fantasy; schools are often viewed as factories or prisons, teachers and students alike act merely as pawns and role bearers constrained by the logic and social practices of the capitalistic system. (p. 259)

Reproductive theories underestimate students, especially women, working-class, and minority students, by portraying them as passive members in the process of reproduction.

Giroux (1983) cites several critical ethnographic studies that contradict this view of students, the most important among them, Paul Willis' *Learning to Labor* (1977). Willis' detailed exploration of male working-class culture in school shows, among other things, just how much working-class students contest and resist domination, even if only to choose, ultimately, a working-class future. This picture of the schools differs greatly from reproductive theories. Far from orderly factories, schools and classrooms are what Giroux (1983) calls contested terrains, "complex and creative fields of resistance through which class-, race- and gender-mediated practices often refuse, reject, and dismiss the central messages of the schools" (p. 260). Reproductive explanations of schools offer little hope for the kind of interaction I've suggested is necessary for an activist pedagogy. Though writing teachers need to be aware of how their own classrooms may participate in reproducing inequalities, to conceive of students as pawns in the system underestimates our students and limits the political potential of the classroom.

An interactive approach to teaching writing, one that allows for student activity and resistance, has both pedagogical and political consequences. Many students are eager to explore ramifications of their social experiences, are eager to document instances of resistance, and are eager to search for the similarities and differences between themselves and their classmates. Just as personal experience essays draw on students' authority of experience and help to build confidence in beginning writers, the essay topics and the analytical papers in this course draw extensively on students' social knowledge, a usually untapped resource of student knowledge. For minorities, women, and working-class students, my course offers a chance to explore background that their educational experience may have led them to see as a disadvantage and a liability. Often, especially by sharing their writing and readings with other students with similar backgrounds, their research leads them to discover common strengths and common interests with those who share their social backgrounds. The conscious exploration and analysis of social backgrounds *with other students* invites students to reinterpret this background as a source of strength. For instance, a woman student had initially understood her language in terms of "powerlessness." After discussing her essays with a woman subgroup member who defined her language as "emotional," not powerless, she then reinterpreted her words to find a more satisfying and more enabling understanding:

> I have heard about how emotional women are all my life. I was never sure if these comments were directed at me or if it's a general concept of women held by many. I used to think anger was just an emotional response, but

anger has given me a form of power. . . . I think women have inherently developed anger as their power. . . . I find that in situations where I have the least power, I often lash out in anger. Examples of this anger are in Essay Three with my co-worker and my father, the sexist teacher who put me down in Essay Four, and at Tom Fox, the teacher, for requiring Essay Ten.

Resistance can take a variety of forms: silence, rejection of the teacher, rejection of the course goals, refusal to legitimate the assignments, rejection of the political frame. More interestingly, as in the case of this student, students can use the political frame itself to voice resistance to discrimination and oppression. Note that her individual and personal experience of anger becomes for her a social and political one. She begins by wondering "if these comments were directed toward me" and concludes, "I think *women* have inherently developed anger" (my emphasis). In the process she transforms a theme of powerlessness to one of potential power. Giroux (1983) stresses that there are a *"range* of oppositional behaviors, some of which constitute resistance and some do not" (p. 285). One feature of students' response to the political frame of this course involves the transformation of "oppositional behavior" to "resistance." The latter contains progressive potential, while the former does not. Anger, for this student, experienced as an individual emotion, "an emotional response," lacks political potential; it is simply behavior that opposes. But reconceived as connected to the place of women in our society, anger becomes resistance, and she transforms herself from passive respondent to active agent.

Note also the anger directed at me. In an interactive classroom, the students talk back, and they talk from a nexus of personal and social concerns, as students wanting to do less work, as women who seek legitimacy, as working-class students trying to move up, as skeptical black students, in short, as people with real concerns and interests that grow from actual life experiences.

Students from social positions of advantage have the experience of understanding the language use of those without those same advantages, advantages they often take for granted. Seeing working-class language, women's language, and the language of ethnic students as purposeful, intentional, and logical can lead to a more tolerant view of diverse groups. Although rarely have I seen the sort of change in students from "advantaged" backgrounds as I've seen in other students, there is a satisfying "truth in labeling" about the language user who admits, "I begin every discussion by stating my opinions as facts" and realizes he gets away with it because he is white and male. At least these students gain an explicit knowledge of their language practices and how they relate to the social location they inhabit.

An interactive approach sees students as active constructors of meaning.

Just as students capably and understandably construct the classroom context, students—by virtue of their age and experiences—are capable readers, writers, and interpreters; they are not passive receivers of text or passive reproducers of written forms or passive receptacles for their teachers' words. I assume, and haven't been proven wrong yet, that the student who reproduces over and over a five-paragraph theme has an understandable reason to do so. Similarly, the student who says "Benito Cereno" is about true friendship (between Babo and Benito!) has a reason and the interactive teacher's job is to find out why. In this case, the student didn't finish the story because she lacked confidence in her ability to interpret. In a section of her final paper devoted to gender and language, she tells about her socialization as the only girl in a family of boys:

> I was never pushed or pressured to do anything—so I didn't! Why put yourself out and try to "be" something, when what I was seemed to be alright for everyone? Except that it wasn't alright for everyone—it wasn't right for me. But I never thought I could do anything, so I didn't try.

Thus her inability to finish the book was the consequence of important social facts about how she was raised, a problem of attitude, social relations, and context, not a linguistic deficit, a cognitive deficiency, a developmental arrest, or a reading problem. The point is not that anything goes in an interactive classroom or that it's fine not to finish the assigned work, but that students can and do make sense, provided they are given the opportunity and encouragement to do it, and provided they know their explanations will be treated with respect, as creations of people with important histories, experiences, and backgrounds.

2
Seeing Teachers as People

Understanding students as people means seeing them as active creators of meaning and context. In an interactive classroom students draw on their social backgrounds to make sense of their language use and to confront their educational histories as students. When students take responsibility for their classroom and their language, where does the teacher fit in? I have indicated briefly, through my discussion of the imposition of the political frame, that I conceived of the teacher in an active, activist role. In defining this role in more detail, I will be drawing on the work of two theorists whose understanding of the role of the teacher has contributed to this study: Paulo Freire's *The Pedagogy of the Oppressed* (1970), and Shirley Brice Heath's presentation of the teacher-ethnographer in *Ways With Words* (1983).

TEACHERS AS ETHNOGRAPHERS

In citing Clifford Geertz's (1973) idea of "Thick Description," I have already invoked the role of the ethnographer. One of the strengths of ethnography, according to Geertz, is its ability to render the "exotic" understandable; exposing a people's culture makes accessible their "normalness without reducing their particularity" (p. 14). In seeking to understand students as people, perhaps not as exotic a task as Geertz's example of a Morrocan sheep theft, teachers can gain a great deal from the attitude of the ethnographer, though ultimately the role has its limits. Shirley Brice Heath has produced an excellent example of "thick description" in her work, *Ways With Words*. Heath spent nearly 10 years as a participant-observer in two small communities in the Piedmont region of the southeast United States. As the title of her book indicates, she was primarily interested in understanding and presenting the functions of language in these communities. Part I of *Ways With Words* is a remarkable example of how ethnography can reveal the role of language (both written and spoken) in a community by attending to day-to-day behaviors. Part II of *Ways With Words* recounts Heath's experience teaching ethnographic techniques to school teachers at a local state university.

Heath's research took place at a historically unusual and important moment, a fact not dealt with at any great length, yet clearly one that she considers a motivating force in her research. She begins *Ways With Words:*

> In the late 1960's school desegregation in the southern United States became a legislative mandate and a fact of daily life. Academic questions about how children talk when they come to school and what educators should know and do about oral and written language were echoed in practical pleas of teachers who asked: "What do I do in my classroom Monday morning?" (p. 1)

To answer these teachers' pleas, Heath conducted teacher-training courses in the use of ethnography as a pedagogical technique. The problem, as Heath presents it, was that both black and white working-class students had styles of language use that inhibited their success in school. The teachers and most of the students in these schools came from "mainstream" culture, the middle classes of the small city near the two communities that Heath studied. The style of classroom interaction favored these mainstream students. Heath's detailed analysis showed, in a manner reminiscent of Labov's (1972) "The Logic of Non-Standard English," that both working-class communities, one black and one white, had complex, rich, and logical—as logical as any—styles of learning and using language. Yet in her words, "[n]either community's ways with the written word prepares it for the school's ways" (p. 235).

Heath understands the task of the ethnographer as does Geertz; she decided that what was needed were "ways to make accessible to teachers an understanding of the differences in language and culture their students bring to their classrooms" (p. 265). Her goal was to bridge these differences by training teachers to become skilled observers of language use, to become in Dell Hymes' (1972) phrase, "ethnographers of communication." They took field notes, visited students' families, learned about language use in students' home environments, and asked students to bring language examples from their surroundings. These teachers began to understand the language use of students who were not from mainstream homes, as the logical product of their home environment.

Even more interesting was that teachers began to understand how their own teaching practices specifically excluded non-mainstream students. A journal entry by one of the teachers demonstrated the type of knowledge these teachers learned:

> The fact that communication is so important to learning points out the need for learning the child's language and also for allowing children to interact and communicate with each other. The very pictures we put on the walls of

the schoolroom show our ethnocentric leanings. Boy was that a slap in my face! (p. 270)

This process of understanding students' language led to the teachers' reevaluation of their own patterns of interaction, of how they based their understanding and evaluation of students on mainstream norms. The teachers then entered what Heath calls the second stage: They began to examine and change their classroom practices to reflect their new respect for diversity in language use. Teachers began to draw more and more on students' home environment for material in reading and writing instruction. One early grade teacher taught the letters of the alphabet by citing the shapes of familiar objects from the students' lives, such as streetlights and telephone poles. Other teachers drew on language in the school environment itself as material and gathered written material (forms, receipts, notices) from the principal, custodian, and lunchroom workers and compared it with examples of writing that students brought from home. As a result of their active use of students' background in teaching reading and writing, teachers became more sensitive to diverse ways of using language and more respectful of language variety. In their roles as ethnographers in the classrooms they became not only better teachers but learners too:

> They learned to believe that their students could learn, and that they could learn from their students. One teacher summarized this feeling: "The needs are many, the motivation is amazing; and the goal of learning from students is for us to know what they have, not to tell us what they lack." (p. 314)

Heath's experience shows that when teachers become learners, they engage their students in a much more significant way than in a conventional classroom. The ethnographer-teacher conceives of students in a way that allows the type of interaction that I advocated in Chapter One:

> [Teachers] did see themselves as engaging students in an *interactive* process in which students learned to share the goals and methods of the classroom as a result of their activities as "ethnographers." (p. 340)

THE GOALS OF ETHNOGRAPHY

The role of the teacher as ethnographer in a language classroom is a "resource" person, trained in the ideas and vocabulary of standard academic experience. When students brought folktales, stories, and the various kinds of language from their home life, the teachers then "helped students to transfer these ways of investigating and analyzing information to the content

areas of science, language arts, social sciences, English, and mathematics"
(p. 339). These teachers saw their roles as "translating" material from
students' home environments into traditional academic subject matters and
language styles. Heath clearly states that the goals of these teachers did
not differ from those of conventional teachers. Although students freely
used resources from their home life, this home life itself was not to be a
subject matter, only a means to a more traditional end:

> The goal of these teachers was not a focus on the collection of cultural
> materials from an ethnic perspective. During the ethnic heritage revival move-
> ments of the 1970s, there were many efforts to collect folk songs, tales, and
> music from ethnic communities for incorporation into classroom routines and
> published materials. The methods and materials described here had no focus
> on ethnic heritage, and the purpose of the ethnographic efforts of the students
> was not to bring their folk culture back into the classroom for memorization
> and study by all the class. (p. 340)

So although these teachers used innovative methods of collecting sources
for teaching and involving students in tasks, they conceived of these methods
in the service of traditional goals. The teachers did not redefine their tasks
on the basis of their new understanding of communities; they did not
abandon "their standards of judging the mechanics of writing" (p. 314);
they did not want to embed the goals of the classroom in a reinterpreted
understanding of the community. Instead, Heath's ethnographers wished to
"translate" or "transfer" the community, more generously understood and
respected because of their ethnographic work, into a traditional conception
of education. We can see this in numerous examples:

> this writing was their own, generated by them for purposes which both met
> their needs and allowed teachers to emphasize school skills of spelling, punc-
> tuation, and requirements of style for different purposes. (p. 314)

> they had to alter their methods of teaching, but not their standards of judging
> the mechanics of writing and clarity of writing. (p. 314)

> teacher's goals were: (1) to provide a foundation of familiar knowledge to
> serve as context for classroom information; (2) to engage students in collecting
> and analyzing familiar ways of knowing and translating these into scientific
> or school-accepted labels, concepts, and generalizations; and (3) to provide
> students with meaningful opportunities to learn ways of talking about using
> language to organize and express information. (p. 340)

Heath did not intend her project to change the structure of school or the
social values surrounding it, nor to change the values of the students.
Instead she wished to enable students from communities whose styles of

language learning conflicted with the demands of the school to succeed in the conventionally defined academic skills. On several occasions, as examples of the success of this program, Heath refers to the greatly improved scores on standardized tests. She also refers to more important results such as students' improved attitudes toward school and better school-community relations. Her program should be seen as a locally-oriented *reformist* one, designed to achieve traditional goals in school by integrating the experience of students who had been, up until school desegregation, excluded from attaining these goals.

ETHNOGRAPHY'S LIMITS

No one should overlook the achievement of Heath's teachers. They involved students and their families in education in an important way, especially since many of these students and families had been traditionally uninvolved. In the "Epilogue" to *Ways With Words,* Heath reports on her interviews with these teachers three years after her study was completed. This epilogue takes its place among the numerous examples of pedagogical experimentations that had temporary effects. The teachers no longer employed Heath's suggestions; "[t]hey wistfully remembered their role in the past as professional creator and critic" (p. 359); they felt that they had become " 'only lackeys in a system over which we have no control' " (p. 359). These teachers reported that, in part, these alienated feelings came from "the loss of many college-bound students to private schools" (p. 359), which I assume to be a by-product of school desegregation, although Heath does not state this. What the teachers' situation represents, though, is the inseparable connection of the communities to the larger system and society. It was this larger society's insistence on school desegregation that initiated Heath's project, and it was the resilient forces of racism, taking white middle-class children ("college-bound") out of the public school because they were integrated, that helped bring it to an end.

Heath's epilogue reminds me of the opening of Jonathan Kozol's *Illiterate America* (1985), and from my point of view, perhaps by default, her epilogue argues for strategies similar to Kozol's. In his introduction, Kozol reports what happened to the children he wrote about in *Death at an Early Age* (1967) since its publication in the 1960's:

> Stephen called me from prison this winter. . . .
> Frederick is not yet in prison. He is a successful pimp. He tells me he deals in drugs. He cannot read. He is not married. He has several children he has never seen. . . .
> Angelina has three children and lives on welfare in the neighborhood where

I first met her as an eight-year-old. She cannot read the Boston *Globe,* advertisements for job, or welfare forms. She cannot read the homework papers of her children. She will not read this book. (p. xvi)

Kozol has as much respect for local understanding and solutions to problems as does Heath. His book is full of moving portraits of actual people in context, though not as thickly described as Heath's. And one of his proposed solutions to adult illiteracy in America is local, grass-roots literacy programs. Yet Kozol's case studies add up to a picture that ultimately is larger than the self-contained communities in Heath's study. Both Kozol's statistical information and his compelling insights into the day-to-day lives of people who can't read or write put literacy squarely in a political context. Educational inequalities, whether on the massive and obvious level that Kozol talks about, or on the more subtle and varied one in Heath's work, are political matters:

When the government itself has been elected by exclusion of one third of the electorate [because they can't read or write], when the third is the third which also gets the most deficient nutriment, least adequate health care, poorest housing, and which has an infant death rate twice that of the middle class, and when that government—having arrived in power—has actively engaged in the reduction of all services and funds which might at least alleviate the pain if not the cause of so much needless subjugation, who can still adhere to the belief that this is not political? (p. 92)

Heath seems to avoid the political issues that Kozol more directly deals with, and yet it becomes impossible for her to exclude these issues totally, for they inhabit the words of the people she studies. *Ways With Words* clearly demonstrates the advantages of the role of the ethnographer, but finally, I find the role too limiting to accomplish the goals I set for the interactive classroom in chapter one.

Mary Louise Pratt (1986) and Linda Brodkey (1987), in separate works, have helped call attention to the conventions and purposes of ethnography. Ethnographic writing seems to call less attention to itself as writing than other genres, in Brodkey's words, "ethnographers tend not to draw the reader's attention to the fact that a story is being told" (p. 71). But Brodkey and Pratt both argue that ethnographies must be as critically interpreted as other genres, particularly if, as Pratt states, we are interested in "changing or enriching ethnographic writing" (p. 27). Pratt goes on to define her purpose:

At times one still hears expressed as an ideal for ethnography a neutral, tropeless discourse that would render other realities "exactly as they are," not filtered through our own values and interpretive schema. For the most part, however, that wild goose is no longer being chased, and it is possible to suggest that ethnographic writing is as trope-governed as any other discursive formation. (p. 27)

In the following discussion of Part I of *Ways With Words*, I will take a critical look at the ethnographer, as Heath interprets it, specifically focusing on Heath's definition of communities, her emphasis on cultural style, and how these "tropes" prevent attention to important social facts in the lives of the people she studies.

Heath lcoates her study historically in the middle of a very politicized event, school desegregation. However, race as an issue, or perhaps better stated, *racism* as an issue, is absent from her discussion of language use. She states the reason in her Prologue:

> This book argues that in Roadville and Trackton the different ways children learned to use language were dependent on the ways in which each community structured their families, defined the roles that community members could assume, and played out their concepts of childhood that guided child socialization. . . . Therefore, any reader who tries to explain the community contrasts in this book on the basis of race will miss the central point of the focus on culture as learned behavior and on language habits as part of that shared language. (p. 11)

Heath argues for an understanding of language habits as a result of a learned culture. In arguing for this point of view, Heath may be trying to counter potential misuses of her book, ones that would seek to find differences based on race that support a negative stereotype or claim that black parents' child rearing habits are responsible for their children's low test scores on standardized tests. Additionally, she may also be arguing for an understanding of language use that allows for more diversity than would a simplistic or invariable understanding of black English. Yet in avoiding these problems, she excludes injustice towards blacks as having anything to do with black or white language use. Though Heath noticibly avoids commenting on racism, conflict, and stratification of race recur as an issue in both the white and black language examples. One citation, concerning the entrance of blacks in the workplace, especially stands out:

> When the niggers (pause) uh, the blacks, you know, started comin' in, I knew that wasn't for me. I wasn't ever gonna work for no nigger—my granddaddy'd roll over in his grave if I did. Blacks takin' up the jobs now, ain't no chance for whites to move up, and I gotta have me a feelin' I can be my own boss for some things. (p. 39)

Heath politely changes the subject after this quotation. But racism won't go away in *Ways With Words;* it permeates the lives of the people it details. Although Heath calls both Roadville (the white community) and Trackton (the black community) working-class communities, Roadville residents clearly live better than Trackton residents. There are no condemned houses in Roadville, no one on welfare, no transients, no alcoholics. Though she says Trackton residents feel marginalized and therefore like a closed community, they also see their hardships in terms of a solidarity with other blacks and "a collective black experience" (p. 67).

Heath's analysis of both Roadville and Trackton stays so close to the idea of a closed community that her analysis deemphasizes issues related to power, privilege, and opportunity. Heath states that the child-rearing habits of Trackton and Roadville do not adequately prepare their children for school. But her analysis shows that hierarchies of social class and race correspond to success in school. Her evidence suggests that Trackton kids have the most difficulty in school; Roadville kids do badly, but slightly better than Trackton kids, and mainstreamers do better than both communities.[1] There appears to be a correlation between wealth, race, and performance in school. Heath would point out that mainstream blacks do better than Roadville whites in school and therefore race isn't the issue. But the fact that race is complicated by class (and vice versa), doesn't mean that it isn't an issue. Do mainstream blacks do as well as mainstream whites? Heath's circumscription of community prevents her from answering these questions. However, her analysis and generous use of examples seem to indicate that language learning habits reflect and reproduce the degree of intervention parents feel they can make in the world outside of their community. Mainstreamers' active intervention in community affairs, including school, corresponds to their focus on "routines and negotiations of intention" (p. 255). Mainstream mothers interpret infants as always meaning something by their noises. They come to teach children a sense of language where one executes self-originating *intentions.* Next down on the hierarchy, Roadville parents focus on "training" their children to learn "and often tell others, the rules they live by" (p. 146). One Roadville resident says, "we grew up with a lot of *shoulds* in our house." Heath connects these "shoulds" with a general pattern of order: manners, traditions, and so forth. Roadville

---

[1] I want to make it clear that Heath does not state that Roadville students do better than Trackton students. But, again, one of the strengths of *Ways With Words* is that her generous use of actual language from Trackton and Roadville residents allows counterinterpretations. A good example of the comparatively low status of Trackton students is Table 8.1 (pp. 268–269). It indicates the negative attitudes that teachers held towards working-class students. Heath separates the teachers' comments about black students from their comments about white students. Although teachers do not regard either group positively, black students received the most negative comments. For a similar view of Heath, see Harold Rosen's (1985) review, "The Voices of Communities and Language in Classrooms."

residents follow and teach these rules, but the rules are not the result of an intention or a decision; they are an inherited pattern. Finally, Trackton residents are playfully fatalistic about raising their children:

> Trackton parents and community members see in each child "the makin's of sump'n," but the way the child comes up and uses these 'makin's' depends on the child. Parents and other adults have limited influence and power over any child: "children will turn out the way they turn out." (p. 146)

I don't think these child rearing practices are ordered on a hierarchy of good and bad—my own preference would be with the Trackton parents— but I do see a hierarchy of confidence in using language to intervene in the world, from the mainstreamers, to the Roadville parents, to the Trackton parents. In all likelihood, this feeling of efficacy in interaction is linked in some way with privileges and sense of opportunity that our social system distributes along the lines of class and race. Heath rightly cautions against any simplistic or deterministic approaches to the connections between race and class and language use, but the fact that no simple connection can be made doesn't mean that such an important social fact as racism doesn't influence language at all. Furthermore, such an exclusion removes the possibility or advisability of collective political action.

Although Heath locates her study in history, her analysis concentrates on *stylistic* differences among Trackton, Roadville, and mainstreamers. Though such stylistic conflicts help us understand Roadville and Trackton students' school performance, without a sense of specific cultural history we get little understanding of the *meaning* of the styles. John Ogbu, in "Opportunity Structures, Cultural Boundaries, and Literacy" (1987a), argues that stylistic explanations are inadequate, for the obvious reason that many minority groups, with widely divergent cultural styles, do well in school-based literacy tasks. Some Asian groups are a good example. Ogbu cites two factors, obscured by a stylistic explanation, that play an important role in shaping language use at school: the perceived labor market, that is do students think success in school will lead to economic stability, and the *history* of the minority culture in relation to the majority culture. American blacks, as well as other "involuntary immigrants," have developed what Ogbu calls "oppositional culture," a culture that defines itself in opposition to the dominant culture. Because American blacks were brought to America as slaves, because slavelike status persisted long after slavery was officially abolished, and because social and economic barriers continue to prevent many blacks from full participation in American culture, the language styles of Afro-Americans, while partially due to African roots (as Smitherman shows in *Talkin' and Testifyin'* [1977]), have developed oppositionally.

Ogbu's work reminds us that style emerges historically, and emerges in a stratified social order. Such a historical perspective is necessary for a teacher to engage in political action. The teacher-ethnographer, in Heath's presentation, seeks understanding and interaction, but does not seek cultural change. This seems consistent with a strict interpretation of an ethnographer, whose job is to inscribe culture (Geertz, 1973, p. 19), not necessarily change it.

Heath's understanding of the political role of the ethnographer basically mirrors Geertz's. At the end of his well-known essay, "Thick Description," Geertz addresses the issue of the political relevance of ethnographic analysis and the danger of lapsing into what he calls "sociological aestheticism":

> The danger that cultural analysis, in search of all-too-deep-lying-turtles, will lose touch with the hard surfaces of life—with the political, economic, stratificatory realities within which men are everywhere contained—and with the biological and physical necessities on which those surfaces rest, is an ever-present one. The only defense against it, and against, thus, turning cultural analysis into a kind of sociological aestheticism, is to train such analysis on such realities and such necessities in the first place. It is thus that I have written about nationalism, about violence, about identity, about human nature, about legitimacy, about revolution, about ethnicity, about urbanization, about status, about death, about time, and most of all about particular attempts by particular peoples to place these things in some sort of comprehensible, meaningful frame. (p. 30)

Although focusing specifically on language use, Heath essentially conceives of the ethnographer's political role in the same way. By choosing to write about a black and white community during school desegregation, Heath has certainly not let her ethnography turn into sociological aestheticism. But neither Geertz nor Heath advocates intervention as part of the role of the ethnographer-researcher. We should not be surprised that Heath's view of the teacher does not seek cultural change, for if ethnography, as Heath and Geertz conceive of it, is taken wholesale as the role model for teaching, then teaching practices will reproduce the culture, not alter it. While techniques of ethnography can usefully enter the classroom to help promote tolerant understanding of diverse language styles, this ethnographic model inhibits teachers wishing to promote social or cultural change. Analysis of the kind that Heath presents in *Ways With Words* may lead to meaningful political action, but it falls into the category of research that John Ogbu, in "Variability in Minority School Performance: A Problem in Search of an Explanation" (1987), labels "explanatory research," which he opposes to "improvement research." Heath's analysis in Part I of *Ways With Words* is a rare and valuable document, taking us into the lives and language of Trackton and Roadville. The question remains, though, of whether *Ways With Words* outlines an ethnography that is appropriate for a teaching role.

Heath's version of ethnography, a tightly circumscribed understanding of community, an avoidance of issues of social stratification, and a basic explanatory stance, is unsuited to the political nature of the role of teaching, limited in its ability to explore and intervene in the serious problems that nonmainstream students face.

A number of researchers in writing, in addition to Heath, have argued that teachers should think of themselves as teacher-researchers. Ann Berthoff (1981), Miles Myers (1985, 1987), Dixie Goswami and Peter Stillman (1987), Glenda Bissex and Richard Bullock (1987) and others have written passionately about the teacher as researcher, and all have also stated that teachers will gain political power by thinking of themselves as researchers.[2] But it seems to me that the pedagogical success, and consequently a political transformation, depends on the kind of research on which teachers base their role.

Recently researchers and educators both have reconceived of the role that ethnography can play for politically active teachers. Roger Simon and Donald Dippo's (1986) introduction to critical ethnographic work, what Ogbu (1987b) would call "improvement research," explores the boundaries between ethnographic work and political action, appropriately beginning, "But is it ethnography?" They define the aim of critical ethnographic work not as simply analysis and explanation, but as critique and transformation. It is both a pedagogical and a political project:

> The pedagogical/political project of critical ethnographic work requires efforts to foster the critique and transformation of unjust and disabling forms of moral regulation and material distribution. (p. 198)

Simon and Dippo's revision of ethnography emphasizes an activist role. Because researchers intervene in the lives of their students, this role is a more appropriate one for teaching, acknowledging a shaping problematic— in the case of this study the role that gender, class, and race play in language use in the classroom. Because of its emphasis on transformation as well as interpretation, the role of the critical ethnographer is one step closer to what Aronowitz and Giroux (1985) define as teacher as "transformative intellectual."

Though not specifically critical ethnographers, Aronowitz and Giroux's conception of the "transformative intellectual," in *Education Under Siege*, fits well with the idea of teacher as critical ethnographer. They argue that teachers need to reconceive of themselves as both intellectuals and as active transformers of history. The need is especially urgent in light of school

---

[2] See Berthoff, 1981; Myers, 1985; and Bissex and Bullock, 1987 (especially Chapter 3) for the most specific discussion on teacher politics and research.

administrators' responses to what the media is calling "the crisis in education," responses that result in limiting teachers' power to determine the conditions of their classrooms. In times of crisis, perceived or real, "experts" step in to solve the problems. The experts usually do not work in the classrooms and therefore do not create solutions that are specifically geared to the historical or social situations of classrooms. Instead of teachers interpreting context, deciding and creating, experts dictate classroom procedures. In worst cases, these solutions involve assignments and even scripts that the teacher must follow. They not only are unable to shape the curriculum for the specific social background of the students, they also remove the human specificity of the teacher. In these "solutions" neither teachers nor students can be fully human.

Literacy, of course, has been at the center of the crisis in education, and one of the solutions developed by the corporate world and taken up by school districts is what Mary K. Healy (1987) calls "Generic Writing Systems." These systems are designed to raise quickly students' scores on standardized writing tests. Healy, like Aronowitz and Giroux, points out the essentially technical character of these programs:

> One of the additional dangers of using a formulaic Writing System is that it centers the teacher's attention on the *system* to be presented—the mechanics and the sequence of it—and not on the learner's attempt to write something with personal meaning. The mechanics of such systems can be initially tantilizing. They present an orderly progression of exercises, and they usually build in attention to some of the clinical teaching directives for modeling and guided practice. They give teachers plenty to do in the classroom—run off materials, then work step-by-step through the packets with students, emphasizing completion of set tasks. Their very efficiency makes it almost impossible for a teacher to adequately follow the directions of the system *and* still have time to look at individual students' interests and needs. (p. 3)

Ultimately, these writing systems reduce the teacher to a mechanical role, implementing the directions of others. As Healy states, it is a "patronizing and debilitating view of what a teacher is and does" (p. 3).

Generic Writing Systems contribute to the more widespread problem of teacher "deskilling." Michael Apple (1983) argues that the process of deskilling separates "concept from execution," and inhibits teachers' ability to make decisions about curriculum and working conditions. Apple explores deskilling by analyzing a science "module," a curriculum system similar to Generic Writing Systems. By breaking down the teacher's actions into small steps (which lead to predefined goals), the science module removes the "goals, the process, the outcome, and the evaluative criteria" from the teacher. By doing so "teachers lose control of the curricular and pedagogic skills to large publishing houses" that manufacture curricular systems. Deskilling makes obsolete the very activities I argue teachers need. We need teachers who interpret, challenge, and sensitively intervene in the lives of their students, but those skills are unnecessary in the Writing System classroom. Literacy, embedded as it is in social and political contexts, requires teachers with skills to interpret and intervene in those contexts, yet Writing Systems, like the science "modules" that Apple discusses, exclude those very skills and reduce teachers' abilities to effect change in the classroom.

Teacher deskilling, educational systems that reduce teachers' humanity and power, the increased influence of experts from corporate publishing houses, technical solutions to human problems all argue for the need for teachers to reconceive of their role in the classroom.

PROBLEM-POSING TEACHERS

Aronowitz and Giroux, perhaps in an effort to avoid prescription, do not specifically delineate what kind of action the transformative intellectual would take in the classroom. My concern in this book is specifically with the literacy classroom and Paulo Freire's (1970) "problem-posing" education provides a more specific idea of the role. "Problem-posing" education, discussed in *Pedagogy of the Oppressed,* shares the ethnographer's focus on the student's cultural background as material for the classroom: "the program content of the problem-posing method . . . is constituted and organized by the students' view of the world" (p. 101). But where the teacher-ethnographers in Heath's book used this cultural background for standard academic goals, Freire seeks to have his students examine their view of the world and transform it. Heath's book challenged the traditional distinctions between teachers and learners, showing how teachers became learners once they became ethnographers in the classroom. Freire also seeks to change the boundaries between teachers and students: "Education must begin with solution of the teacher-student contradiction" (p. 59). But again, Heath's teacher-learners wished to change roles so that they could better understand how to help students succeed in traditional classroom tasks. Freire seeks to change the teacher-student relationship to facilitate the students' critical understanding and transformation of society. There is no doubt in my mind that the skills of ethnography can be profitably used by Freire's problem-posing teachers, but these skills would be used in an activist pedagogy, one that seeks understanding and change, not just understanding. Freire's pedagogy has an explicit political intention: the liberation of oppressed people. He developed his pedagogy in Brazil teaching in literacy programs. In these programs Freire saw language teaching as revolutionary activity; he was successful enough that he was jailed by Brazilian officials. The change that Freire reports in his students is not just in their ability to read and write, but in their sense of themselves: from passive receivers of experience, people who felt that things happened to them, to people who felt they could actively intervene in the world around them to change it. By "naming the world," Freire's students enter into it, and become "increasingly critical and thus less alienated" (p. 69).

I want to emphasize the difference in context between Freire's Brazil or Chile, or programs that have duplicated his results on Indian reservations or urban centers in the United States, and my study.[3] Students in Freire's programs volunteered in "educational projects," grass-roots organizations separate from the "systematic" education, funded and governed by the state. His students are clearly oppressed members of society, and more or less completely illiterate. My students are mostly from middle and upper levels of society; they were required to enroll in my course; state universities are surely "systematic" education, and my students entered my course with reading and writing abilities adequate enough to get along in society.

This difference in context makes simply transferring Freire to the United States inappropriate. Still, when Freire wishes for his students to critically understand their "situation," when he asks them to "name the world," these goals do not differ so much from my aim to have students reflect on how their social background affects their language use, and by doing so, take responsibility for the way they use language. Though all my students were literate, many students did not "name their world" in the sense Freire means, nor did they feel unalienated from their language. In Chapter Five, for instance, a student refers to her own writing as "like an enemy." This understanding of students' needs demands interpretation and intervention and makes a role such as problem-posing a relevant one for the teacher to take in my context.

Problem-posing teaching begins with the students' presentation of their own experience, what Freire calls the student's "thematic universe." The teacher's task is to present the students' situation back to them as a problem. Students then need to understand the situation again, this time actively and in a dialogue with another person:

> The task of the dialogical teacher . . . working on the thematic universe revealed by [his or her] investigation is to "re-present" that universe to the people from whom he first received it—and "represent" it not as a lecture, but as a problem. (p. 101)

In my course, the political frame of the categories of gender, class, and race represents the contours of the "problem" I posed to my students. I

---

[3] For discussion of some of these projects see Nan Elsasser and Vera P. John-Steiner (1977).

posed this problem not only in the structure of the course, with its requirements to do analytical papers concerning these topics, but in everyday discussion, conferences, and comments on their writing. I have discussed, in Chapter One, why gender, class, and race functioned as a problem.

How does a teacher pose problems? As an example of problem-posing, I want to look at comments on written work as one illustration of the dialogue that goes on between problem-posing teachers and students. In understanding the role of written comments, I have also been influenced by Lil Brannon and C. H. Knoblauch's (1982) article, "On Students' Rights to Their Own Texts: A Model of Teacher Response." Brannon and Knoblauch argue persuasively that by telling a student "how to do a better job" teachers appropriate the student's text. In Freire's terms, these comments function to "narrate" the reality for the student (and education, according to Freire, is suffering from "narration sickness" [p. 57]). Evaluative comments, positive or negative, not only appropriate the text, but also obscure the students' understanding of their own intentions:

> the teacher more often than the student determines what the writing will be about, the form it will take, and the criteria that will determine its success. Student writers, then, are put into the awkward position of having to accommodate, not only the personal intentions that guide their choice-making, but also the teacher-reader's expectation about how the assignment should be completed. (p. 158)

In a memorable passage from *Letter to a Teacher,* included in Ann Berthoff's *The Making of Meaning* (1981), the Schoolboys of Barbiana lampoon evaluative comments from a similar position as Brannon and Knoblauch, but punctuated with sarcasm. They claim that paper comments "are all nothing more than assertions." In the following passages they first give examples of teacher's comments (in quotation marks), and then follow these comments with their own remarks:

> "Childish. Infantile. Shows immaturity. Poor. Trivial."
>
> What use can a boy make of this sort of thing? Perhaps he should send his grandfather to school; he's more mature.
>
> Other comments: "Meager contents. Poor conception. Pale ideas. No real participation in what you wrote." The theme must have been wrong, then. It ought not to have been assigned. . . .
>
> Then we also meet the creature touched by the hands of gods: "Spontaneous. Rich flow of ideas. Fitting use of your ideas, in harmony with a striking personality." Having gone that far why not just add: "Blessed be the mother who gave you birth"? (Berthoff, 1981, p. 203)

The Schoolboys of Barbiana, Freire, and Brannon and Knoblauch argue for commenting that does not bless or condemn, but engages students in a learning dialogue.

In the courses I taught for this study, I responded to my students' writing in the nonevaluative, dialogic manner suggested by Brannon and Knoblauch, Freire, and the Schoolboys of Barbiana as one way of posing problems to the students. My usual pattern in paper commenting is to begin the dialogue by summing up my understanding of what the student has presented and then follow with a question designed to reconceive the student's experience in terms of the social categories of my course. The questions are sincere, not rhetorical, for during the course neither the student nor I know the ways in which these social categories affect his or her language.

For instance, in response to a student who said she identified with Mrs. Hale in Susan Glaspell's "A Jury of Her Peers" (1918) because she was also a woman and the "men in this story were such jerks!," I responded:

> In this essay you identify with the women in a story which, as you say, portrays men as "jerks." Certainly, to empathize as you did [with the women], you are familiar—at least from a distance—with "jerks." Knowing there may be potential jerks in your audience—how do you adapt your language? Do you? In what way do you write with other women in mind? [all essays may be reproduced for the class as a whole]

Another example: A student cited the passage from *Life in the Iron Mills* (Davis, 1861) where Kirby says, " 'I have heard you call our American system a ladder which any man can scale. Do you doubt it? Or perhaps you want to banish all social ladders, and put us all on a flat table-land,— eh May?' " (p. 34). The student went on to explore the two "sides of the economic system that [he] was raised with." He then related experiences from his life that demonstrated either the ladder system where people "climb," or "slip," or the flat table-land system, which he interpreted to mean "caste system." He then expressed his view that the ladder system more accurately described our economic system, and said he felt confident in being able to "move up." Here are my comments:

> I underlined all the "action" verbs. They are often used by others, like Ronald Reagan, in defending "free enterprise" because a basic feature of the system is that anyone with confidence and courage, someone willing to take action, can achieve success.
>
> "Confidence" is an important value in language use, too—obviously this is both a personal feature of yours *and* a cultural value. What is the relationship between confidence and social class? How does it show up in language?

These comments illustrate the basic pattern that I outlined above. The first part restates in my language what the student has already said. In the above examples, I quoted or cited words or passages that the student actually used, the first student's identification and reason for it, the second student's use of action verbs and confidence in his language use. I see these initial features as part of my effort to understand the student's context. In the next step I take the restatement and make it into a problem by relating it to the political frame. I don't see these comments as either nondirective or authoritarian. I certainly am asking students to consider their language in specific ways. In the first student's case, I ask her to understand how gender roles influenced her response, and I implicitly ask her to compare her rhetorical strategies with her interpretive strategies in "A Jury of Her Peers." In the second student's case, I ask him to scrutinize his use of action verbs and gain a more complex understanding of the relationship between social class and confidence in language use. Although I certainly pose problems in a directive way, these are not rhetorical questions, nor could they be. I did not know the answer to the question, "In what way do you write with other women in mind?'" Nor did I know how the second student would understand the role of social class in confident language use. In fact, in the second case, I wasn't entirely sure if there was a relationship.

These comments were meant to engage students in a dialogue, and while this dialogue certainly has a purpose, defined mostly by me, students had to construct their own answers. I posed the problem, itself a directive move, but the solution had to come from students. In actual practice, this is a delightfully unpredictable process. I have learned to form my expectations very tentatively; students sometimes refuse to answer my comments at all or answer them in a way I would have never conceived. For instance, the second student's final paper restates "confidence" in language as an economic strategy designed to counteract the unfairness of the ladder system:

> A person at the bottom of the economic ladder will be afraid to stand up for what he feels is right, because he feels someone higher up on the economic ladder will contradict him. And once he is contradicted, most people will accept the viewpoint of a person higher up on the economic ladder rather than vice-versa. So, the person toward the bottom of the economic ladder will not be heard, and his viewpoint will be considered wrong. If this occurs over and over again, the person toward the bottom of the economic ladder will become less and less confident.

I really didn't expect anything to ensue from my comment—it was one of 15 I'd written to this student. I also didn't expect this particular answer. The two important points about these examples are: The student actively constructs an answer that the teacher doesn't know, and the student understands the teacher as a person with a point of view, asking questions and posing problems sincerely without knowing the solution.

THE PROBLEM WITH POSING PROBLEMS: HISTORY REVISITED

There remains a crucial problem in writing these kinds of comments, the problem of students' histories of experience in the classroom. Just as students' experiences shape their understanding of their own roles as Students, their experiences also shape their conceptions of the role that teachers can take. Despite being as conscientious as possible in writing nonevaluative comments, in reviewing my course evaluations I find how little my intentions matter and how powerful are the influences of students' historical understandings of teachers. I often received evaluations that indicated that I achieved the goal of my commenting, such as this one: "I found your comments very beneficial and consider them a vital part of the learning that is achieved in this course. It made the writer think of why he wrote the way he did." But I also found evaluations like these: "A good way to spot flaws in specific areas," and "I think that this [paper commenting] is extremely helpful in finding out what you think is appropriate" (immediately after this comment, this student revealingly wrote "I do feel that a grade of some sort (number 1–10) anything might help one to become more aware of where he/she stands in the class").

That students read comments that I intended to be nonevaluative as evaluative is not due to my lack of skill in writing nonevaluative comments. Students expect comments to be evaluative because of their common experience in classrooms. Students entered my classroom having spent roughly 12 years in the classroom. These years come to shape what a teacher is and can be. Alfred Schutz and Thomas Luckmann (1973), using Schutz's work detailing "social reality," has called this shaping force of experience "typification." Schutz's point is that people do not proceed randomly from situation to situation experiencing each one freshly, but proceed from one situation to the next building up a series of perceptions and expectations that are put to use in understanding new situations. These experiences eventually become entrenched (Schutz calls this the "sedimentation") and they begin to *shape* new experiences. For a situation to break from a well-established norm, something radically different must occur, for minor changes (like nonevaluative commenting) are likely to be reinterpreted in light of the original "sedimentation."

No doubt my students have received thousands of comments on their written work, which, however politely stated or well-intentioned, were evaluative. My students interpreted my actions on the basis of a "typification" of teachers in general. Schutz has elaborately described interactions between people in terms of varying degrees of "typification." In relationships where we have frequent face-to-face interaction, such as with family members, one understands and expects behavior that is typical of a unique person. For instance, my sister behaves typically like the individual who is my sister, and this typification is not transferable to other people. Some typifications Schutz calls "functionary," meaning that we base our relationship on getting a specific task done and we understand and evaluate the relationship in terms of this task and not, say, on the personality of one of the partners.

Students construct their teachers not on the basis of a unique face-to-face interaction, but on the basis of a type whose function is to transmit knowledge and evaluate students. Freire articulates the features of this typical teacher in his description of the "banking concept of education," where teachers are involved in the task of "depositing, in which the students are the depositories and the teacher is the depositor" (p. 58). Students in my class expect to have knowledge about language, writing, and literature "deposited." They expect my assignments and papers to be a good opportunity to show the teacher what a good job they have done *recounting* the deposit.

THE POLITICAL TEACHER

The question I will now turn to seems awkwardly already answered, but because it is such an important question, I would like to spend some more time answering it: Is the activist teacher, one who imposes problems on students, an authoritarian teacher? In light of the above discussion of how students' educational histories shape their understandings of teachers and students, one can see that even if the activist teacher differs from this history, the imposition of politics can always be reinterpreted by students in light of a more traditional intent.

Still, the question of authoritarianism is a good one and a necessary one. When this question is asked, usually by those who don't share the politics of the activist teacher, it is usually asked from a point of view that imagines that a teacher can be apolitical in the classroom. But the difference between an activist and a teacher who would not be called an activist is not one between a teacher who teaches politically and one who does not. Richard Ohmann (1976), better than anyone, has shown how political values and intentions have always been in the English classroom, and how claiming their exclusion itself functions politically. His best example is New Criticism, which remains the most powerful pedagogical model for teaching literature. Teachers teaching in the New Criticism style taught students, in Ohmann's words:

close reading—exactness, sensitivity to shades of feeling, the need to see
pattern and order, the effort to shut out from consciousness one's own life-
situation while reading the poem, and to pry words loose from their social
origins. . . (pp. 70–71)

Critical practices in the classroom always do more than teach styles of
reading, and New Criticism taught more than close reading, for surely there
are values in such practices; there are assumptions about the goals of
reading, about readers and writers and language use. Such values in New
Criticism, argues Ohmann, support a flight from politics, prefer individual
thought to collective action, and individual freedom to responsibility for
others (pp. 77–91). The label "activist" does not then mean one who teaches
politically, but one who acknowledges political intentions.

In some sense then, everyone is a political teacher. This fact, while true,
does not justify authoritarian teaching, it points out that everyone enacts
politics in the classroom, and activist teachers admit it. The difference between
an activist and an authoritarian teacher is not one between one with politics
and one without, but involves the relationship between specific politics and
teaching styles. The specific convictions that I mentioned in Chapter One—
promoting tolerance and enlarging the opportunities of oppressed groups—
don't easily lend themselves to authoritarianism. Not all politics are equal,
even if acknowledged. Teaching students to hold a conviction of tolerance,
for instance, is not a process that can be accomplished in Freire's "banking
concept" of teaching. Students don't become tolerant by having the concept
"deposited" in their heads, or being told that if they aren't tolerant, they'll
get an "F." Such methods do teach students politics: Individual efforts will
be rewarded by a hierarchical power structure; if students behave like
Students, they'll get an "A."

Where does that leave an activist teacher? I want to return to Freire's
description of the banking concept, and this time look at the role of the
teacher. Freire sums up the teacher's role in the banking concept like this:

(a) the teacher teaches and the students are taught;
(b) the teacher knows everything and the students know nothing;
(c) the teacher thinks and the students are thought about;
(d) the teacher talks and the students listen—meekly;
(e) the teacher disciplines and the students are disciplined;
(f) the teacher chooses and enforces his choice, and the students comply;
(g) the teacher acts and the students have the illusion of acting through the
    action of the teacher;
(h) the teacher chooses the program content, and the students (who were
    not consulted) adapt to it;
(i) the teacher confuses the authority of knowledge with his own professional
    authority, which he sets in opposition to the freedom of the students;

(j) the teacher is the Subject of the learning process, while the pupils are mere objects. (p. 59)

While no teacher would want to admit to being a banker, making deposits in his students, shouldn't the teacher teach? Shouldn't the teacher think? Shouldn't the teacher talk? In sum, shouldn't the teacher be an active Subject? Aronowitz and Giroux's (1985) contention that teachers need to be transformative intellectuals in the public sphere needs to apply also to their everyday behavior in classrooms. Freire's point is not that the teacher and students should change places, and that teachers should become versions of banking students. The goal in problem-posing teaching is to allow both students and teachers active roles in learning, to become *"co-investigators"* (p. 97). The trick, of course, is to manage the active role of teacher without making passive students, to teach, think, talk, and choose without preventing students from doing the same things. The function of posing problems helps accomplish this goal; students need to actively develop and create solutions. Ultimately, I wish for students to develop the habit of posing problems, the habit of critically questioning their experience.

SEEING TEACHERS AS PEOPLE

Perhaps the most important step that the individual teacher can take to disrupt the typification of the banking teacher is not to grade. Because of institutional and departmental constraints, most teachers do not have this option, nor was not grading an option for the classrooms in this study. Yet it is clear to me that grades, even when postponed until the final draft, represent the most obvious means of maintaining the typification of the teacher, constantly simplifying the relationship between student and teacher to one of compliance with and rebellion from the teacher's demands. As the case studies show in Chapters Three through Five, there are as many ways to comply with and rebel against the teacher as there are students. Yet I cannot overstate the importance of this grading in the shaping of the responses in this course. Schutz claims that the experience of the "natural attitude" of daily life is pervasively determined by a *pragmatic motive* (p. 6). For my students, the pragmatic motive is to get an "A" or to pass the course, and largely and inescapably the writing in this study can be analyzed as strategies to get a good grade.

I tried to pose students' attitudes towards grading as a problem, complicating their strategies to get a good grade by (a) announcing that if students complete the work, I would give them a "B," (b) not grading the essays, even in my comments (see discussion of paper comments above), (c) not grading the analytical papers, (d) not giving a midterm grade, and

(e) telling the students that I was not even grading them "in my head." For some students these strategies did seem to affect their work; honest appraisals of confusion and confessions of occasional laziness indicated to me a relaxation of the teacher typification. For the most part, though, the final grade overwhelmed all these strategies. The most successful strategy was to announce that the context of grading itself should be an active part of students' analyses of their responses. Here are my directions on a handout for the final paper: "In your final paper, you should honestly and frankly consider the effect of the teacher, your classmates and the course structure (including grading) in shaping your writing." The "should" in the previous sentence should be read as "should in order to get an 'A'." This strategy worked to a degree because it placed one typification in conflict with another. Typically students and teacher both ignore the issue of compliance in order to maintain the more flattering (to both sides) ideal of the pursuit of knowledge. Students don't normally claim that they are motivated by the desire to get a good grade, much less analyze the secret business of such a motivation—their means to get an "A." My injunction to study the effects of the grading is a clear command, that good Students should follow. All of these strategies made it more difficult, though not impossible, for students to maintain the typical stance toward the teacher.

The obvious solution to disrupting students' typification of teachers as bankers is to behave like a person and not a type. When students are people, they have social origins, experiences, concerns, and interests. Why should we deny teachers these same qualities? For teachers to avoid authoritarianism, they need not abandon their experience, expertise, interests, or goals. But instead of attaching these qualities to an abstraction of the Teacher, these qualities need to be seen as attributes of a person. For a classroom to really be interactive, the teacher has to contribute actively too.

One day, after spending an hour-and-a-half in a particularly frustrating departmental committee meeting, I walked into my classroom with an exasperated look. One of my students asked what was wrong and I explained that I was on this committee and I was getting fed up with "conservative professors." Another student, Ms. Y, a member of the Young Republicans on Campus, said "What's wrong with being conservative?" All of the class saw this as a challenge, for I had described my politics in my first essay, which I distributed to the class in the same fashion as I distribute my students' essays. My reply was that I did not have time to enumerate all of the things that are wrong with being conservative, but we might take this occasion to explore what being conservative means in Ms. Y's language use. I had fortunately duplicated two of her essays for discussion. To open the discussion, I asked, "How can you tell that Ms. Y is conservative from just looking at her writing?" I honestly expected a blank silence, but instead, after a few minutes (seconds?), students were talking vigorously. They named a great number of features: a sense of independence and individuality (students characterized these attitudes as "I'll decide for myself" and "I'm only responsible for myself"), and a wealthy background (indirectly—for she mentioned "travel," "waterskiing" and she didn't mention "work"), among other features. The whole discussion was punctuated with challenges by the students as to whether or not a feature such as "individuality" really meant conservative, or even what we actually meant by conservative. Ms. Y, ever capable and confident, participated fully and defended herself when necessary and agreed in general. She realized, through this impromptu study of her language, as did the class as a whole, how attitudes shaped through experience in a class structure, for instance, affected her writing.

The discussion was, in part, initiated by my own disclosure of political convictions early in the class, and more immediately initiated by my frank admission of emotions activated by a political confrontation. A similar point with regard to teaching is made by Evelyn Torton Beck, in "Self-Disclosure and the Commitment to Social Change" (1983). Beck claims that becoming a human being in the classroom works to achieve political goals. First, she advocates an active role of the teacher:

> self disclosure humanizes the teacher and makes her more accessible. Thus, self-disclosure reduces the student-teacher hierarchy without undermining the fact of the teacher's expertise. (p. 162)

Beck also claims that self-disclosure promotes the kind of tolerance I seek to develop in my classroom:

> self-disclosure gives the teacher the opportunity to validate diversity and difference in terms of race, class, age, sexual preference, and ethnic origins, among other things, some of which are less easily categorized. (p. 162)

By presenting myself as having experiences that help explain my language use, my mood that day, my course and its aims, my teaching style, and my political opinions, I am inviting students to engage in similar acts.

This kind of discussion engaged in by Ms. Y and her classmates, a spur-of-the-moment explosion of exploration, is vital learning. When such an explosion occurs, suddenly English becomes important enough to argue about. It can only happen with students who are confident people in the classroom. And they are confident because they are in a classroom with a teacher with expertise, experience, and authority—but one who is above all a person like them, with a history, goals, and politics.

Introduction to the Case Studies

The following case studies continue my analysis of language use in the classroom. Case studies have the advantage of presenting information about students in a form that corresponds to the ways teachers experience students. Unlike statistical comparisons or holistic generalizations, case studies, with their attention to details (Geertz's "thick description"), can convey the sense of a real student with both idiosyncratic and typical features, one who actively participates in the classroom context and disrupts or confirms teachers' expectations. Since I focus on possible political consequences of an interactive classroom, a particularly important advantage of case studies is their ability to document change and progress through time.

I chose these students' work to examine because it seemed particularly well-suited for illustrating the interaction of social backgrounds and language use in the classroom. However, I did not conceive of these students as representative, in the strict sense of the word. Readers should not look for the essence of male and female language in Chapter Three, nor for a perfect example of working-class language use in Chapter Four, nor for typically black language use in Chapter Five. The categories of gender, class, and race seem to invite stereotypical understandings, but these cases in particular and my study in general argue against them.

There is nothing either predictable or predictive about these case studies. The students vary considerably in their willingness to explore their backgrounds, in the way they understand and present themselves, and in the degree of change they expect to take place as a consequence of my course. Three of the four case studies examine students whose backgrounds are not socially privileged: a woman, a working-class student, and a black student. Although some of these students' strategies of using language are similar, I could draw no general conclusion about them. Even if I could make these conclusions, the value of this information would be limited. As I have stated in Chapters One and Two, teachers and students continually create the classroom context, influenced by important historical expectations. The political frame and an activist teacher challenge these historical expectations and students respond to the challenge in an endless variety of ways. If I wished to propose a generalization about these cases, this generalization would apply only to these students in my course; it would not apply to other students in different courses, nor to the same students next month or next year, nor to other students in my class with the same social background.

What use are these case studies? How do they help understanding how social group membership affects interaction in the classroom? The first point that these case studies show is the strong shaping power of social identity. Once given a chance to explore the connections between their social histories and their language use, students created original and convincing explanations. One can see, in these students' essays, how considerations of gender, class, and race influence every aspect of the classroom, from the more unusual demand of the political frame to more conventional concerns about grading and evaluation. In every way of using language, interpreting stories, writing informal essays and formal papers, or interacting with small group members, students richly and meaningfully explained their ways of using language through the lens of their social backgrounds.

There is no need (or basis) for me to draw conclusions or make predictions of how the categories influence language use. Instead, they create the plausibility for the connections between individual and actual student behavior and these larger, politically important categories. To use Geertz's phrase, these cases provide "sensible actuality" to my presentation of students and teachers as people. Because I convey the information through the work of my students, the force of the argument is made by retelling actual student's language use instead of by making generalizations.

These case studies will be most valuable for those who wish to create an interactive learning context. Yvonne Lincoln and Egon Guba (1985) call this criteria of value "transferability." The ability of a case study to "transfer" depends on its "fittingness," which is the "degree of congruence between sending and receiving contexts" (p. 124). Although also concerned with how the specific categories of gender, class, and race affect these students' language use, together the case studies continue the argument made in Chapters One and Two, an argument for a pedagogy that will incorporate social backgrounds of students in language study. Even with fitting contexts, similar classrooms with similar goals, these analyses will have to be repeated by each student in every classroom because contexts are recreated (shaped, as always by history) in actual interaction. Gender, class, and race matter in language use and the following case studies suggest how and why they matter.

3
Gender Interests in Reading and Writing

The two case studies in this chapter illustrate the effect of students' respective experience as men and women on their language use in the classroom. These two students, one male and one female, used language in quite different ways. Ms. M carefully monitored her language to make sure she didn't offend her audience of peers. Mr. H, on the other hand, wrote freely with intensity aiming to persuade his audience to agree with him, focusing on the teacher as his main audience. I am aware that the two case studies in this chapter could support an existing stereotypical conception of men's and women's language. These stereotypes portray men's language, as "forceful, efficient, blunt, authoritative, serious, effective, sparing and masterful," and women's language as "weak, trivial, ineffectual, tentative, hesitant, hyperpolite, euphemistic" (Cheris Kramer, cited in Spender, 1980, p. 33). These stereotypes not only differentiate language on the basis of gender, but clearly stratify it, too. Men's language is superior and women's is inferior.

These case studies do not support this damaging dichotomy. They do not "represent"—symbolically, typically, or in any other way—an acontextual men's language or women's language. Instead, each case shows how social conceptions of gender work to shape the way these students express themselves in my classroom. Ms. M's "hesitant" language strategies, for instance, more accurately represent an intelligent survival strategy than an indication of weakness. And her tendency to censor controversy more accurately represents her commitment to the classroom community, a characteristic far from "trivial." Although I believe that many students have had experiences similar to Ms. M's or Mr. H's, and that competition or self-consciousness about appearance may result in similar language uses in other students, I don't intend these essays to predict language use.

Stereotypical predictions of language use ignore the important shaping power of context and, worse, underestimate people's ability to vary their language creatively according to their perception of context. Conclusions about the relationship between gender, reading, and writing need to be situationally specific, for neither men's language nor women's language is stable across contexts. Feminist language theorists, such as Dale Spender

(1980) and Patricia Nichols (1983), show that women's language varies considerably from context to context, and one of the variables of this context is whether or not men are present. Ms. M's own reports suggest that *only* when her language was for an audience of men and women peers was her language unsure or hesitant. She suggests that had her subgroup been composed of all women students, her essays would have been much different (she doesn't say how). As it was, her subgroup included the confident and authoritative Mr. H.

As Ms. M's tentative and hesitant language strategies seemed to confirm a stereotypical "women's language," Mr. H's confident and authoritative style may seem only to confirm a typically male language. But, as with Ms. M's language, Mr. H's rhetorical and interpretive strategies need to be tied to the social context. Mr. H's authoritative style was influenced by his understanding of the classroom, and his particular understanding of the student role as competitive. His small group members were both women; he seized the role of leader in the group, and perceived himself as leader in the class as a whole. These actions, in turn, were also motivated by his wish to succeed as a student (to get an "A"), which meant impressing me and paying less attention to the response of his audience of peers.

As my analysis will show, these language strategies and their relationship to the context complicate any simple characterization of men's or women's language. By showing how these strategies result from deep-seated, gender-related social habits, my analyses of these students' language argue against an easy evaluation of these stereotypical language strategies, against a conception of women's language as somehow deficient and men's language as superior. Instead, I present both sets of language strategies as an understandable result of the social arrangements of men and women in our society. An evaluation of the advantages or disadvantages of either set of strategies has to be made within this context and any change in language will be accompanied by a change in the student's perception of the context.

Neither Ms. M's language strategies (especially at the beginning of the course) nor Mr. H's seemed perfectly satisfactory; I hoped both students would benefit from my course. The same feature of contemporary gender roles hinder both: contemporary society not only defines men and women separately (they are different in kind), but also defines men and women hierarchically (they are different in value). Mr. H's confident strategies, assumed by him because of his location in the sex/gender system, ignored for the most part the sensibilities of his peers, especially the two women in his subgroup. For this specific audience, his writing did not achieve the kind of effectiveness he wished for. Ms. M's habit of monitoring her language for offensiveness prevented her from enacting some of her important values in communication, although the habit increased her sensitivity to her audience of peers. So, certainly, evaluation and change are in order. But this kind of language change can't be mandated by a teacher's corrections or evaluative comments. More substantial change comes from the process of understanding the relationship between gender and language that the student herself or himself undertakes. One can see, particularly in Ms. M's work, the beginnings of such a change.

BEAUTY AND "THE BIRTH-MARK"

I am going to begin explicating Ms. M's work with an essay she wrote in response to Nathaniel Hawthorne's "The Birth-mark" (1974). The initial point I will argue is that, as a reader, Ms. M constructed, understood, and identified with Georgiana, the woman character in the tale, on the basis of her own experience in socially constructed gender roles. These roles, as everyone knows, have different characteristics associated with them; the crucial one to begin the study is beauty. Differing attitudes toward beauty in men and beauty in women in our culture may at first seem to be only an example of the social separation of gender, but as my analysis will show, the examination of beauty in Ms. M's response leads us to understand how beauty functions to *stratify* men and women as well and leads to a more general understanding of Ms. M's language use.

Ms. M wrote the following response in a freshman composition course in 1984 in answer to the question, "Read Hawthorne's 'The Birth-mark.' Tell which character(s) you most closely identified with and which character(s) you identified with least."

(1) In Hawthorne's "The Birthmark," I would have to say I most closely identified with Georgiana. I say this because she was very self-conscious about her looks, which is a feeling I think everyone experiences to a certain extent. There seems to always be something that a person feels self-conscious about, whether it be a big nose, large thighs, one's weight and even a birthmark.

(2) Georgiana had a birth-mark, which resembled a little hand, on her cheek. This really had not bothered her until her husband mentioned that it took away from her total beauty. She then became more and more self-conscious about it, as her husband seemed to become more obsessed with getting rid of it.

(3) When a loved one tells you they do not like something about you, it hurts much more than if a stranger or an acquaintance had said the same thing. This is because you want to be appealing and pleasing to the one's you love or are closest to.

(4) I can identify with this because if someone I really care about tells me something I could do to improve myself, whether it deals with looks or

personality, I take the suggestion to heart and try to follow through with it.

(5) I have trouble identifying myself with Aylmer. I believe that if you love someone enough to marry them, you should accept them as they are and not want to change their looks. After all, she had her birthmark before they were married and he did not appear to have said anything to her then. Besides, what counts the most is what a person has to offer from the inside, not from the outside. If anything, he should have tried to make her feel more comfortable about it. Instead he became obsessed with getting rid of it and would shudder at its sight. This of course really hurt her feelings and made her constantly aware of it. I think he should have shown more consideration for her feelings. . . .

(6) One similar feeling to Georgiana's that I have experienced, is the fear of being rejected by the people you care about. For instance, in high school there was the pressure of wearing the right clothes and acting a certain way in order to be accepted by your friends. This pressure also exists now, but seems less emphasized.

(7) Another feeling similar to hers is the feeling of self-consciousness. When I had glasses I was very self-conscious about them but became even more so when my friends and family told me I would look better without them. So I ended up getting contacts later . . . (here, as elsewhere, the elipses are mine)

I want to pursue two explanations: the second dependent on the first. The first is a reflective explanation, showing how cultural or social values are reflected in Ms. M's conception of herself and her interpretation of "The Birth-mark." The second explanation is motivational, explaining why Ms. M interpreted "The Birth-mark" in the way she did by exploring how the social context acts on her and how she acts on the social context. I define the social context as both the immediate classroom and our patriarchal society. This motivational explanation shows not only how cultural values are reflected but also how they are reproduced. Through this aspect of the explanation students gain the potential to change.

The most prominent cultural value Ms. M refers to in her identification with Georgiana is women's concern for beauty. "Self-consciousness about looks" seems to be the means by which Ms. M constructs her understanding of Georgiana. We can sense the importance that the concern for beauty plays in Ms. M's life by, first of all, her sympathetic understanding of Georgiana's character. She did not respond to Georgiana by dismissing her as "a puppy dog," as one woman student did. On the contrary, Ms. M said she "closely" identified with Georgiana, and understood her actions because self-consciousness about looks is "a feeling everyone experiences to a certain extent." Although she doesn't specifically mention Georgiana's death, Ms. M does indicate that there is an emotional price in attaching this importance to beauty. She indicates this emotional price by the negative feelings she associates with not looking beautiful: "hurt" (paragraphs 3 and 5), "fear" (paragraph 6), "pressure" (also paragraph 6) and the intensity of her statement that she became "even more" than "very self-conscious" (paragraph 7).

It is interesting how thoroughly issues of gender relations are missing from Ms. M's account. The references to women and men in this essay are all genderless: "everyone," "loved one," "someone," "people," "friends," and "family." The fact that Ms. M does not see beauty as a gender issue also reflects the culture Ms. M inhabits. Robin Tolmach Lakoff and Raquel Scherr's uneasiness about even considering beauty a topic for their book, *Face-Value: The Politics of Beauty* (1984) testifies to the fact that our society considers beauty a private concern, not a social one, and certainly not a political one. Beauty, according to Lakoff and Scherr, was "not at all something you brought up as a serious thought in public. It was what you agonized about privately" (14). One can see by the examples of physical characteristics that Ms. M claims to be self-conscious about, especially "large thighs" and "one's weight," that self-consciousness about looks *is* gender-related. But in Ms. M's public response statement she reflects the cultural habit of isolating beauty from the context of gender relations.

But, of course, beauty, in our heterosexist society, does exist in relationships between women and men. Concluding her research in "Gender Difference and the Production of Subjectivity," Wendy Holloway (1984) states that in our present society "being attractive means being attractive to the opposite sex" (p. 241). The fact that Holloway utters this common-sensical notion at all reveals the extent to which discussions extract beauty from its socially-constructed origin. Only through examining this social construction can we come to understand Ms. M's response to Georgiana as motivated, for motivational explanations concern themselves with relations between people.

Ms. M's concern for beauty, or "self-consciousness about my looks," intertwines with what she introduced as her main theme in all her essays. In her thesis statement from her final analytical paper, Ms. M states:

> Wanting my writing to be accepted and liked by my audience, not just any audience, but one which is made up of my peers, is the theme of my essays.

Ms. M's thesis statement bears on a motivational explanation because it clearly places her language use in a relationship with peers. I find Ms. M's concentration on peers a bit unusual for a student in a graded course, yet the following explanation, also from her final paper, remains consistent with my understanding of her language use:

> if I were writing for you only [me, the teacher] I might not think things out
> so thoroughly, by this I mean I might not weed so many things out which
> I think may seem dumb, silly or weird to my peers. Instead I would be more
> carefree with my writing, because if you as the teacher rejected what I wrote,
> it would be my writing you were rejecting and not me as a person. My peers
> on the other hand, would be rejecting not only my writing, but me also.

The fear of rejection is the same explanation Ms. M used to support her
understanding of Georgiana in the essay I quoted earlier, and she connected
this fear of rejection with the necessity of wearing the right clothes for her
peers.

Rejection, anxiety, and fear accompany Ms. M's notion of beauty and her
theme of wanting to be accepted and liked by her peers. These feelings
indicated to me and to her a sense of powerlessness which she characterized
as "lack of confidence" in her writing and interpretation. Ms. M's concentration on her peers as audience, and her construction of them as potentially
rejecting her as a person, led her to censor any topic which would give her
audience material to reject:

> I do not want to arouse any anger or bring up anything controversial because
> I want everyone to like what I like. Earlier I stated that I did not want to
> offend anyone in my audience, which is true, but now I am saying I do not
> have the confidence to offend anyone in the audience.

This gave her writing, especially her early essays, a vacant quality which
another student in his analysis of her essays described as "elusive."

This elusive or vacant quality ties in with the cultural stereotype of
beauty, that beauty and intelligence are mutually exclusive. Ms. M's blond
hair and the cultural myth of the "dumb blond" reinforced this stereotype.
Cultural myth and the reality as experienced by Ms. M parted, however,
when the audience changed from her peer group to me alone. I have indicated
that I found Ms. M's first essays unimpressive. She seemed uninterested in
engaging serious topics. When I received her first analytical paper, which
was not duplicated for the entire class, her perceptiveness, honesty, and
depth of understanding astounded me. Ms. M explained the difference in
her discussion cited earlier about writing to peers and to the teacher, but
she corroborated this explanation with the following statement from her
second analytical paper: "I know more about what is going on than the
people around me sometimes think." She reveals, in this statement, a habit
of public deportment that is silent, skeptical, and keeps important knowledge
private. This stance prevents her from actively using her knowledge in the
public arena. The following quotation from her third analytical paper places
this habit in the context of gender roles: "Women in our society tend to

take the passive role in that they defer to men's ideas and tend to keep theirs hidden inside."

What does this have to do with beauty? It reveals, for one thing, Ms. M's understanding of the hierarchy of cultural values for women; beauty is important, daring intelligence is not. Furthermore, Ms. M is also conscious of the penalty for demonstrating too much intelligence, the threat of being seen as "pushy, aggressive." Ms. M finds herself, then, in a difficult situation. She is intelligent and yet a cultural prescription inhibits the expression of this intelligence. Ms. M's experience reveals what sociologist Dorothy E. Smith (1979) calls the "line of fault." According to Smith, the line of fault occurs between reality as experienced by women, and reality as legitimated by the dominant social group (men), between "experience and the forms in which experience is socially expressed" (p. 135). For Ms. M, she experiences her intelligence, yet also understands that in a patriarchal version of "reality," she would incur penalties for expressions of intelligence.

In dealing with this "line of fault," Ms. M comes up with the following strategy:

> I do not usually give a definite idea or belief of my own, so the reader never really knows where I stand. Instead, I write my ideas and opinions through someone else in my essay. You could say this is a protective device I use.

The interesting term, "protective device," suggests her understanding of the need for protection from a potentially hostile audience and also reveals a high level of consciousness about her language strategies. These "protective" strategies operated in the realm of "public discourse," that is, only in the essays that were to be duplicated for the entire class. They also characterized her verbal behavior in her subgroup, a small group of three students who met regularly (every two weeks). This subgroup included Mr. H and one other female. Ms. M describes her participation in this group in the following passage:

> I tend to hold back in my essays and in the subgroup, I never just write something down, I think about whatever I am going to write and if necessary, I make it come across as being less offensive or strong. I also do this in the subgroup. At times I start to blurt something out and then I hold it back, thinking I might be wrong or it may be offensive to someone in the group. This shows a lack of confidence and fear of being rejected by members in the group. However if we are talking about something which I do have a definite feeling or opinion about, I do say what it is. Yet, I still find myself trying to be careful what I say. This makes me angry with myself and I ask myself "why do not you just say exactly what you feel or think."

Considering the above observation, we can understand the gender-based construction of some of Ms. M's other interpretations. For instance, Ms. M's understanding of Janie in *Their Eyes Were Watching God* (Hurston, 1978) seems constructed on the type of gender relations that Ms. M experienced in subgroup. The most important episode in the novel, according to Ms. M, occurred when Janie "thrust herself" into the conversation of her husband and his friends (p. 117). Ms. M cites this passage as evidence of Janie's "spunk" and "guts." Seen in the light of Ms. M's behavior in subgroup and in class, this passage may also represent a goal or a model for Ms. M: an example of a woman who successfully risked the penalties of speaking out in a male-dominated discourse. This response also places Ms. M's practice of "never letting anyone know how much I really know" in the context of gender:

> [Janie] is saying that men think they have everything figured out including women, because they consider women to be inferior. But little do they know, women know much more about what is going on than men think. This comment has to do with the way I am because a lot of the time I know more of what is going on than the people around me sometimes think.

Ms. M relates her tendency to be silent in public groups to gender relations where men consider themselves to be superior. Ms. M's construction of literature needs to be seen in a more complicated way than a Hollandesque recreation of identity. Ms. M's understanding of the story is situationally specific, motivated by the context of a mixed-sex audience and a set of social habits that devalues women's talk. Ms. M's term "protective device" proves this point; there would be little point writing "ideas and beliefs through someone else" if she didn't fear her audience's negative judgment of her own discourse. I don't mean to suggest that if, for example, Ms. M's audience were all women, somehow we would see a more "true" version of her interpretation, one free from "fear of rejection." Certainly, a different context would produce a different reading, but one is never free from a context, and the new one would also exert force.

One can see Ms. M's "protective device" in her identification with Mrs. Peters in Glaspell's "A Jury of Her Peers" (1918) on the basis of the now familiar characteristic: "she knew more about what was going on than she told." When one thinks of the comparison with Janie's action, Mrs. Peters' decision to conceal the evidence from "the men" seems very similar to how Ms. M understood Janie's "butting into" the conversation of the men. Both women characters, like Ms. M herself, begin as "observors" and not "participators," but in the course of the story, take action. In a parallel way, this development describes Ms. M's behavior in my class.

Ms. M's observations about her verbal behavior in subgroup and class discussions underscore her insight into her reading strategies and her written language use. Dale Spender, in *Man Made Language* (1980), describes women's language use in public discourse in terms strikingly similar to Ms. M's. Spender says that contemporary gender relations consistently deny women "the confidence to express and affirm the validity of their own experience" and thus women "employ protective strategies" (p. 87). These strategies, according to Spender, are the same ones Ms. M employs: silence, indirectness, hesitancy, and a tendency to monitor expressions closely.

Spender asserts that these features of women's language have their source in the fact that men control and dominate public discourse. Many language theorists have asserted this, including Robin Lakoff (1975), Barrie Thorne, Cheris Kramarae, and Nancy Henley (1983), and others. We can best understand Ms. M's particular experience by looking at the particular public discourse of her subgroup as reported by the three members. Mr. H, the one man in the group, states that Ms. M and the other woman subgroup members "are both indecisive and write whatever pops into their heads," both "write unauthoritatively and with little confidence," and he describes these qualities as stemming from fear: "It is the fear of being wrong that motivates their quiet and unauthoritative behavior." Although the women in the subgroup both mention "fear" in the context of the subgroup, it is not the fear of being wrong, but rather the fear of being rejected. Ms. M's hesitation in speaking freely stems from "a lack of confidence and a fear of being rejected by the members in the group," and the other woman states: "I have a fear if I stand up or try to lead I will be shot down or laughed at by others." One can see in this subgroup how broad social divisions are reproduced in actual, local situations, how Ms. M's protective strategies function in both a cultural context and a specific classroom context.

Ms. M's understanding and articulation of her "protective strategy" points not only to her intelligence but also to her ability and willingness to "beautify" her responses and writing for her audience of peers. For in the absence of a legitimated space to express intelligence, beauty takes its place. Lakoff and Scherr's witty analysis of the relationship between beauty and intelligence helps to illuminate Ms. M's strategies:

> until recently and perhaps still too often, a woman who wanted the sort of success society unambivalently allowed women—success in love, 'catching' a successful man—had to play dumb. And the more intelligent someone is, the quicker she is to learn important lessons. If there were indications that men preferred women who were beautiful but dumb, why, she'd not only figure out how to be more beautiful than anyone, but more dumb as well. (pp. 37–38)

Ms. M appears to have learned her lessons well. Though she could have learned them anywhere in our culture, she cites her father as the one who taught her "never let anyone know how much I really knew. . . . By doing this, he said, I would always be one step ahead." While her father meant it as well-intentioned advice, it also gives her only the type of power or control that is dependent on the behavior of others: passive, not active. This explains Ms. M's reliance on beauty as a means to power, for beauty provides the exact same sort of power, in Lakoff and Scherr's words, "Beauty's power depends on its possessor being considered beautiful by others—a passive accomplishment—and power is not, of necessity, passive" (p. 41).

Ms. M's identification with Georgiana, thus understood in the two over-lapping contexts of a patriarchal society and a specific classroom, demon-strates how "The Birth-mark" comes to be, as Judith Fetterly says in *The Resisting Reader* (1978), "a parable of woman's relation to the cult of female beauty" (p. 26). By explaining how this meaning results from her own internalized social values, and by developing consciousness of how these social values help shape her language use, Ms. M gains the potential to change. Her conscious understanding of the relationship between gender-related values and writing and interpretation would, perhaps, lead to a more confident self-presentation, one that would be less dependent on "passive accomplishments." She began this change near the end of the course; even Mr. H noticed it, for he wrote: Ms. M "seems to have become more confident and open in her writing; consequently, her input in subgroup has also increased." I would have enjoyed a longer pedagogical relationship with Ms. M to see how this consciousness would affect her future language use. But quarters and semesters conspire to limit our ability to see substantive change. Smith sees the conscious articulation of "the line of fault" as the first step towards social change. Ms. M seems to have taken that step.[1]

COMPETITION, PERSUASION, AND MASCULINITY

Ms. M's subgroup member, Mr. H, provides an instructive contrast to Ms. M, one that will illuminate the gender-specificity of her work, just as the previous analysis of her essays will help to define the role of masculinity in Mr. H's essays. While Ms. M bases her language strategies to a great extent on making sure she does not "offend" her peers, adapting her

---

[1] Ms. M's case study was included in an article of mine entitled, "Method and Gender-Related Motives in Reading and Writing," originally published in *Forum in Reading and Language Education* (October 1986), pp. 57–78. I am indebted to the responses by Egon Guba, Carole Edelsky, and Patrocinio Schweikart that follow the article. Edelsky's response helped generate revisions of this manuscript (particularly in Chapter Two). Schweikart reads Ms. M's work as motivated by an "ethic of care" (echoing Gilligan [1982]), stressing a positive side to Ms. M's identification with Aylmer. See Edelsky, Carole, "A Response to Fox," *Forum in Reading and Language Education* (October 1986), pp. 85–92; Schweikart, Patrocinio, "A Response to Fox," *Forum in Reading and Language Education* (October 1986), pp. 93–102.

language to fit others' expectations, Mr. H organizes his language strategies around persuasion, getting others to adapt to his point of view:

> In my sub-group I am the leader. I begin every discussion by stating my opinions as facts. The other two members of sub-group tend to sit back and agree with me . . . I need people to agree with me.

Mr. H begins from a position of power: "I begin every discussion by stating my opinions as facts," and proceeds in such a manner that he consolidates this power: "I feel more confident when I am an authoritative figure." Such emotions, Mr. H's confidence and authority on one hand, Ms. M's fear on the other, along with the effect these emotions have on language use, underscore the importance of the social roles that students bring into the classroom and enact during the class.

Mr. H's participation in subgroup and his essays in general reveal a sense of self, one that acts to change himself and other people, that seems entirely distinct from Ms. M's sense of self, dependent on and related to others. Even though Mr. H sees the masculine role as problematic, he consciously constructs himself on it:

> Males are traditionally raised to be tough and independent, not showing their emotions. They are also thought of as natural leaders. I personally have lived by this definition and it caused problems in my life. I need to be a leader, but I used to never show any emotion.

The first point I want to explore is the "tough and independent" qualities mentioned above. These qualities are traditionally masculine ones, but what I find interesting is that Mr. H presents these qualities as products of his individual self. For instance, in his third essay, Mr. H describes a time in his life where he *chose* to become "tough and independent":

> I personally used to be an open and very nice and sensitive person: deep down I still am. However, through competition with my family and relationships at school, I changed my personality, 'toughening up' and shutting others out.

Mr. H presents this "toughening up" as an active, conscious choice, something he decided to do: "I changed my personality." Note that it involves creating a sense of independence ("shutting others out") and that it is in response to what he perceived as competitive relationships at home and at school. Characteristically, Mr. H presents himself as autonomous, self-controlled, master of his self and his surroundings. This sense of self reveals a distinct contrast to the "fear of rejection" expressed by Ms. M.

Competitive relationships at home and at school, the sources of Mr. H's "tough and independent" self, represent a central preoccupation in Mr. H's essays, beginning with this statement from an essay written on the first day of class: "I am an intensely competitive person." In the essays that followed, Mr. H discussed competition and conflict with fellow cadets at West Point where he spent a year, with basketball teams and officials, with schoolmates, and most importantly, according to Mr. H, with his brother. Mr. H alluded to his rivalry with his brother several times in his essays and in conversation. He finally wrote about this relationship (with characteristic intensity, I might add) in the last essay written for this class. This essay, a response statement to Hemingway's "The Doctor and the Doctor's Wife" (1925), required an analogy to the student's own history. Mr. H began his analogy with a story about losing his temper in a basketball game, but it quickly develops into an intense discussion of his family:

> My parents treated me as if I were a spastic child that always lost his temper. This was not true; it was as if I was a caged animal being ruthlessly provoked by others outside the cage. My brother and sister loved this game of provocation and played it to the best of their abilities. I would often times get violent, but only when provoked. It was after such instances that my fellow family members would blame the situation on me. I had lost my temper. . . . It was unjust and unfair. . . . To this day my parents don't understand me. I went off and joined the Army while [my brother] remained the family angel, what a travesty. [My brother] goes to school here. . . . He often times takes drugs and wastes his God-given talents. If my mom could only see her little angel for what he really is. I have accomplished more things in my life and reached more goals than my brother and sister; yet, I am still the one that loses his temper.

Most notable, of course, are Mr. H's clearly articulated anger and indignation. But at this point I would first like to note the sense of competition in Mr. H's language. First is the comparison between his "goods" and his brother's, "the family angel." Mr. H compares the relative worth of himself and his brother: his brother wastes his "God-given talents" while Mr. H makes use of them (in essay 1 he states, "God gave me a healthy mind and body and it is my responsibility to get the most out of both"). Mr. H has accomplished more "goals" than either his brother or sister. Compare this sense of competition and related anger and indignation with Mr. H's essays concerning his experience at West Point. He introduced the subject on the first day of class:

> I am an intensely competitive person and I enjoy playing sports. Playing division one basketball was a dream come true when I accepted a basketball scholarship to the United States Military Academy. However, I found that basketball at the college level was no longer fun, it was an extremely hard job. In addition,

placing me in the military was like placing oil on water; the two components just don't mix.

Just why the "dream come true," college basketball, was no longer fun for this "intensely competitive person" was made more clear in a later essay. In citing the most important passage in *Their Eyes Were Watching God* (Hurston, 1978), Mr. H cites an episode where the male protagonist, Tea Cake, overhears a conversation between Janie and Mrs. Turner, a black woman who "can't stand black niggers" (p. 210). Mr. H identifies with Tea Cake in his hatred of Mrs. Turner and then goes on to draw an analogy with his experience at West Point:

> I never fully understood the system at West Point. I was supposedly part of the young men and women that were the best America has to offer. The so-called "cream of the crop." Why was I then being treated with such prejudices and as a fourth rate human being. What was harder to understand and more frustrating was that I was being degraded and stripped of my pride by people who once were in my same shoes and who belonged in my same race. This race: we were all West Point cadets. Just as Mrs. Turner was a black woman who thought that she was better and superior to darker negroes; older cadets thought that they were better and superior to me. This frustrated me and I hated the Mrs. Turners at West Point.
>
> Cadets that two months previous to my entrance to the Academy were fourth classmen now were third classmen and thought they were that much better than me. I was actually hated by some people because I was just starting my career at West Point and was a fourth classman. I was called "smack," because that is the sound shit makes when it hits the wall and that was all I was; a pile of shit. I was literally a slave to the upperclassman and had to do whatever they requested. . . .
>
> No person's better than me and I am no better than any other person.

The same sort of anger and indignation indicates the similarity between this essay and essay 10, concerning his family. And here, too, Mr. H presents a world of competition. Mr. H examines his own worth and finds himself to be part of "the cream of the crop." At the same time he criticizes the upperclassman for their hypocrisy, similar to the critique of his family situation expressed by the phrase, "what a travesty."

This comparing and competing stems from Mr. H's perception of an unjust description of himself as a "spastic child" or as "smack." He understands these definitions of himself as externally imposed by people in a superior position, upper classmen or parents. These senses of self that Mr. H presents reveal a contradiction or a conflict in the picture of Mr. H as a confident and authoritative person, a person with a sense of autonomy, self-control, a feeling of mastery over the self and his surroundings. In the essay concerning West Point, as in the essay about his family relations, Mr. H tells of a set of social relations where he is far from any "sense of mastery" and clearly at a disadvantage in a social hierarchy. Both essays demonstrate the resultant emotions Mr. H characteristically reports in his responses: anger and indignation. Both passages also show Mr. H's ability to dramatize effectively his feelings of unjust subjection; he says, increduously, "I was *actually* hated." He also exploits the shock value of his nick-names, "smack" and "spastic child." These essays were not atypical for Mr. H, for several of his essays told stories of confrontation, frustration, embarrassment, and failure.

A reflective explanation, one that shows how social relations are reflected in Mr. H's reading and writing strategies, could explain how Mr. H's language use reflects the standard, or characteristic, language habits and values of males in a patriarchal society. But a reflective explanation could not explain why, in nearly half of his essays, Mr. H presents himself as disadvantaged by a more powerful social hierarchy. Ms. M characterized Mr. H's typical rhetorical stance as that of "the underdog." How do we explain the contradiction between a confident self-presentation and a series of self-portraits which show Mr. H to be embarrassed, degraded, and occasionally out of control?

Although Mr. H claims to enjoy "competition," his experience in his family and at West Point were in hierarchies that allowed him no possibility to reach the top. Successful competition at West Point depended less on individual effort than institutionalized seniority, thus no self-originating strategies, like deciding to be "tough and independent," could change his position. Mr. H's family situation seems similar: His brother has the same kind of "seniority" that Mr. H, no matter how good his grades are, cannot displace.

The issues of hierarchies in Mr. H's essays relate to an oft-repeated sentiment, Mr. H's concluding statement in essay 7, quoted above: "No person's better than me and I am no better than any other person." Mr. H uses this motto in two characteristic ways. The first is a defensive one: The motto works to justify his anger at being put into a position of unjust subjection. By asserting his "real" equality, he legitimates his intense anger. The essays concerning West Point and his family exemplify this first use of the motto. The second use of this motto relates to my opening characterization of Mr. H as "tough and independent." In this second sense of the motto, Mr. H constructs a democratic ideal where each person is independently responsible for his or her own fate; success or failure depends on making use of one's own equal and independent resources.

This second value is central to his interpretation of "The Birth-mark." Like Ms. M, Mr. H identifies with what he sees as Georgiana's "insecurity," but he clearly points out that his identification ends with Georgiana's final submission to Aylmer. Ms. M understood Georgiana to have gone along with Aylmer's schemes because she wanted to be "appealing and pleasing" to the one she loved. Ms. M's construction of Georgiana recalls her own rhetorical strategies in the classroom; she constructs her language to be appealing and pleasing to her peers. Mr. H, on the other hand, constructs the explanation for Georgiana's action on "insecurity" and "vanity." The difference is crucial. In Mr. H's version, Georgiana is responsible for her own fate: "In the end, her insecurity led to her death" and "Georgiana's vanity led to her death." Aylmer escapes mention and blame in Mr. H's essay. Note that Mr. H's understanding of Georgiana also reflects his characteristic rhetorical stance; Georgiana's failure was a failure to persuade, a failure to change her surroundings. Her death was not due to Aylmer's schemes, but Georgiana's surrender: "Georgiana did something that was very wrong" when she submitted to Aylmer. He contrasts her behavior to his own: "Although I was insecure . . . I changed to a more domineering personality." And Georgiana should have, too. Unlike Ms. M, who sees Georgiana in a relationship where she is at a disadvantage, Mr. H assumes that Georgiana has the same resources for change and action that, for example, Aylmer has. Like the androcentric sociologists discussed by Dorothy Smith, Mr. H takes for granted "the power to act and coordinate in a planned and rational manner and to exercise control as an individual over conditions and means" (1979, p. 150).

Mr. H takes a similar view of Janie, the protagonist in *Their Eyes Were Watching God* (Hurston, 1978). His view of Janie early in the novel is similar to his judgment of Georgiana: Janie, he states, "did not have the security or will 'not to bow down' " and thus she was like people who "bring prejudices upon themselves by *allowing* other people to control them. It is their responsibility not to let this happen, but live the life they so desire and not create prejudices against themselves." When Janie's life turns for the better, he credits her: "It was Janie's refusal to 'bow down' that gave her the personal happiness and freedom she so desired."

Mr. H's focus on the phrase "bow down" reveals his acute sense of hierarchical relations, even while positing a democratic ideal of equal resources and responsibility. Interestingly enough, this democratic ideal remains only an ideal; it hardly ever exists in either Mr. H's personal essays or his construction of literature. In fact, the opposite is the case. Mr. H states that "there is an authority figure of some kind . . . in all of my papers except one." And really, Mr. H's essays are a litany of hierarchies, from the graduations of classmates at West Point, to his description of a basketball game where the official unjustly penalizes the player, to the way he presents his family as a hierarchy of privilege with his parents at the top, followed by his brother, then sister and then Mr. H. All of these hierarchies work to Mr. H's disadvantage, and as he states, in a marvelously appropriate misspelling, they "inferiorate" him.

In his interpretations of literature, Mr. H characteristically constructs hierarchical situations and identifies with characters who are disadvantaged by the hierarchies. For instance, he claims to identify with Aminadab in Hawthorne's "The Birth-mark," a character with two sentences to his name. Aminadab is in a clearly delineated inferior position to Aylmer. Mr. H cites the narrator's comment that Aminadab is "incapable of comprehending a single principle" of Aylmer's research as the reason for his identification. In "A Jury of Her Peers," Mr. H identifies with the timid Mrs. Peters after she tells of the time when she was suddenly and seriously enraged when a boy brutally killed her cat. In his essay on *Their Eyes Were Watching God*, Mr. H, unlike the majority of white students, constructs the story on the basis of race relations, and in his analogy he compares his situation at West Point to Tea Cake's station in Mrs. Turner's hierarchy of color: "I was an underclassman at West Point, in fact a plebe, the lowest of all. I was a fourth class person just as Tea Cake was in the darkest and lowest class of negroes." Mr. H's literary interpretations have in common with his personal essays a construction of authority that unjustly and unfairly exploits sympathetic characters.

So here's an interesting situation: Mr. H proclaims an ideal of democracy in his essays, represented by the phrase, "No person's better than me and I am no better than any other person." Yet again and again Mr. H presents a world of hierarchies where he is consistently at a disadvantage. Mr. H claimed there was one exception to the pattern of authority figures frequenting his work. By way of explaining the above paradox, I would like to examine briefly this exceptional essay (#2), written in answer to the assignment: "Tell about an instance where someone said (or wrote) something that seemed to you to be characteristic of the opposite sex. Explain your relationship to the other person and why you thought it was typical of the opposite sex:"

> Since the beginning of high school, when most girls start carrying their first purse, there has been one phrase I always seem to hear: the identical phrase my old girlfriend would say to me, "It's somewhere in my purse but I can't find it." This is only typical of the opposite sex. I have yet to see in my short life a real organized female, let alone an organized purse.
>
> There is something about a female's purse that amazes me. I would not be surprised to find a S.O.S. pad or a kitchen sink amongst all the compacts, lip gloss, calendars, brushes, and God only knows what else. How can so much stuff be crammed into such a small bag. It has to defy at least one of the laws of physics. Even more fascinating is how a female can find at least one of the items she so often hunts for. A disorganized purse is only typical of the opposite sex.

Although this is the essay that Mr. H cites as the one that doesn't contain a hierarchy, it appears to me that the hierarchy is certainly present, but unrecognized by Mr. H because he, for once, is not disadvantaged by it. And the hierarchy is, of course, male/female. Mr. H presents women as anthropological *objects* under the writer's scrutiny, thus the term "female," instead of the more familiar "girl" (which he begins with). He characterizes women as unpredictable and strange. They "amaze" and he finds them "fascinating;" moreover, they defy the laws of physics. Implicitly, the rational, organized man (with the laws of physics on his side) contrasts favorably with the disorganized and inefficient "female."

Mr. H feels no need—or motivation—to claim or recognize that this essay presents a hierarchy, because if there is a hierarchy then he benefits from it, instead of, as is usual in his essays, being victimized by it. These masculine values of rationality and organization are the same values that he uses to describe his own habitual language system, language use that is motivated in reaction to the unfair hierarchical structure of his family, peers, schoolmates: "It is the anger of being a victim of authority that motivates my language system. . . . Not anger in a radical sense, but organized, well constructed and productive anger." So while Mr. H usually wrote of violent, angry confrontations, he did so in an "organized" and "well-constructed" manner. He frequently employed the language of a scientist (and a behaviorist at that): "I am a highly intense individual and when provoked by a certain stimulus I will respond a certain way." The language of the rational scientist serves to legitimize Mr. H's angry and confrontational self and considerably augment his own authority, even while he presents experiences where he does not have this authority. Mr. H's strategy in subgroup and in class discussion, stating his opinion as facts, certainly relates to this role, for the scientist inhabits the world of facts.

When Mr. H constructs the language system of his subgroup member, Ms. M, he does so on the basis of these socially constructed gender roles. He claims his language is rational and organized, while he claims that the women members "write whatever pops into their heads." He also says that during subgroup meetings, both women more or less speak and write spontaneously; he makes the following generalization: "Girls tend not to think in the long run, but rather in the present. They often talk and write what pops into their head at the spur of the moment." This description, despite being the very opposite of Ms. M's own report, works to his own advantage in two ways: The first is in terms of content—organized and rational is "better" writing than disorganized and irrational writing; the second is that by stating that her writing is "spontaneous," he thus escapes his responsibility for his participation in the context. In other words, if Mr. H were to understand her language use as "silenced" or "muted" or "censored" then he would have to confront his own responsibility for it.

While Ms. M's language strategies seem to be dominated by her perception of her classmates as the most important audience, Mr. H's language strategies seem not to be that simply arranged. Mr. H states that he writes with "the basic need to fit into [his] peer groups" in his first analytical paper, but this theme drops out in the later analytical papers in favor of a more accurate formulation: "My confident and authoritative writing—it is motivated. I personally need people to agree with me." The difference between "fitting in" and "needing people to agree," I believe is gender-related. At the very least it reveals a striking difference between a writer who sees her purpose as flexible, depending on an audience whose beliefs she constructs as fixed (she will fit into what already exists) and a writer who feels he can change the existing beliefs of the audience by his confident, rational, and authoritative style. Seen in this light, Mr. H's use of profanity, and his expositions that present himself as unjustly degraded, exemplified by the nickname, "smack," rely on a audience that would have to agree with his indignation for his writing to be successful. The response is supposed to be, as he explains, agreement. In the essay about West Point he certainly did not expect his audience to think (as I did), "Well, what did you expect, isn't that what the military is supposed to be like?" In relying upon this agreement, Mr. H demonstrates a self-worth that seems indestructible—he certainly does not expect to be called "smack" in this class. His presentation of self in writing and speech, his conception of the rhetorical and social context (they are the same), all indicate the type of language user who is, above all, confident that he can secure agreement.

On whom does Mr. H rely for agreement? Who is his audience? Elisabeth Daeumer, in "Gender-Bias in the Concept of Audience" (1985), explores the language use of a male student who describes his language in terms of rhetorical strategies designed to " 'grab' or immediately 'seize' the reader's attention" (p. 35). Daeumer concludes that, despite being asked to consider class composed of mostly of women students taught by a woman teacher as his audience, her student maintained the fiction of a male audience, and "subsumed his female audience into a generalized male reader" (p. 36). Daeumer's careful analysis leads me to explore the extent to which Mr. H's rhetorical strategies of persuasion are related to his conception of audience. In essay 2, Mr. H's language use seems clearly to be directed towards a male audience—what woman, even with the mock-anthropological stance, would be persuaded to agree that women are disorganized and inefficient? I would have to conclude, with Mr. H's use of profanity in written language and the above essays, that Mr. H's writing is characteristically intended for a male audience. For Daeumer's student, this shows the strength of "the androcentic bias of our culture which leads us to perceive 'man' as the norm" (p. 40), but the case is different for Mr. H, because the teacher is also a male.

So rather than an abstract male audience, Mr. H seems to have conceived of me as his primary audience. The teacher-student relationship discussed in Chapter 2, one where the teacher is a problem poser and not an evaluator, contributed to Mr. H's language choices. Mr. H claims he "felt comfortable in this classroom and safe to write the papers I did. Had I been in another class with a different professor I would have been hesitant to write such papers as the ones dealing with my feelings at West Point." The hierarchy of the classroom is fundamentally different for Mr. H from the ones he cites at West Point, among blacks in *Their Eyes Were Watching God*, or among his siblings. The difference is that the above hierarchies are between members of the same class—"cadets," "blacks," "siblings"—and the teacher-student hierarchy is one which is between two classes that Mr. H recognizes as differentially privileged. Mr. H's competitive drives occur between members of the same class for the prize given by the member of the class in the next hierarchy—officers, whites, parents, teacher.

Mr. H was as active and dominant in class discussion as in his small group and he frequently began discussion in the class as a whole with his familiar strategy for gaining authority: "By leading discussion and presenting my opinions as facts, I feel I can persuade the class as well as the teacher to agree with me." The competitive motive to be the best among students was clearly to achieve excellence in the eyes of the teacher. Mr. H was the only student to quote my handouts in his analytical papers, treating me as an authority: "It has been stated by Tom Fox that. . . ." And even his admission, "The class atmosphere motivated me to write honestly; not for the teacher to the degree as in other classes, but for myself. I did not write a certain way to please Tom Fox, I wrote the way I felt," while certainly true to some degree, is itself an example of "writing to please Tom Fox," because that is exactly the kind of thing I like to read. I don't mean to put Mr. H in a double bind—he writes for the teacher if he does or if he doesn't—but to point out how he constructs a rhetorical situation in which he can write for himself *and* for the teacher in a way that Ms. M, for instance, clearly could not. Because I was a male teacher, and because Mr. H was a man comfortable with public discourse in ways that women students rarely are, Mr. H could unify his purposes in writing. He was able to write for himself, for the class, and still write for the teacher. For Ms. M, however, there was an irreconcilable conflict between writing privately for the teacher and writing publicly for the class.

The conflict or contradiction between Mr. H's acceptance of the standard masculine role of "tough and independent" and his portrayal of a self victimized by hierarchies has a socially legitimated stylistic solution. Unlike Ms. M's concern for the social penalties of a woman speaking out in public, Mr. H has at his disposal accepted linguistic means to overcome his disadvantage. Mr. H effectively dramatized his unjust subjection by rational and objective language. He can present his anger and indignation and assert his rights in a language that is socially acceptable for men. Here is how Mr. H describes his general theme:

> My language system and writing reflect past experiences and emotions in my life. I write the way I feel and often look upon my life with anger. Anger directed toward my home life, especially the relationship I have had with my family. Not anger in a radical sense, but organized, well constructed and productive anger. A special drive, a motivated source to become the best, rises above the misuse of authority that so often haunts me.

The sense of competition ("motivated source to become the best"), the anger at subjection, the sense of confidence in language use ("I write the way I feel"—and I think he means it), all are products of the ideology of masculinity. Mr. H's tough and independent self needed to be constructed in order to compete and survive in the world of unjust hierarchies. Competition, in this sense, requires self-motivated individuals, and inhibits because the prize (parents' favor, teacher's grade) is so dear—careful consideration of a nonevaluating audience's feelings. Mr. H's understanding of the rhetoric of persuasion is thus born of competition, not adapting one's language for an audience, but "winning" the audience's agreement.

Mr. H freely speaks of the cost of this ideology, noting that he "used to be an open and very nice and sensitive person," but changed by "toughening up" and "shutting others out." The intense essays about his experiences at school, West Point, and home, the real sense of anxiety, anger, and pain associated with the perception of himself as a caged animal, a spastic child, or as "smack," all bespeak the costs of masculinity as Mr. H defines it. They are certainly real costs, but Mr. H's "language story," as he told it in my course, was a success story in his terms in a way that Ms. M's was certainly not. Mr. H, with his intense competitive drive, the anxious emotions, could "tame" his provoked animal self, order the movements of a spastic child, and rise above the shame of "smack" by adopting assertive and masculine language conventions of rationality, persuasion, and objectivity.

4
The Rhetoric of a Working-Class Student

In the last chapter, we saw how Ms. M's social understanding of the relationship between women and public discourse affected her presentation in my class. In order not to see her early vacant or elusive writing as indicating a fundamental deficiency in her linguistic ability, we had to understand this writing in the double context of a patriarchal society and my classroom. In this chapter, I will continue exploring how student writing occurs in a double context. The context of the classroom, of course, remains; in addition to that context, we will focus on how a class society, as perceived and constructed by a working-class student, Mr. C, affected his reading and writing in my class.

As in my discussion of gender and language, I want to avoid the stereotypical conceptions of class and language that present working-class language as somehow deficient. One of the sources of this stereotypical understanding is Basil Bernstein's (1977) early formulation of his theory of restricted and elaborated codes. Briefly, restricted codes, broadly related to the working class, are characterized by short, grammatically simple sentences (little subordination), small vocabulary, and simple use of conjunctions. Elaborated codes, broadly related to the middle class, are characterized by complex syntax, expanded lexicon, unusual adjectives and adverbs, and passive verb forms. This formulation has been highly influential and frequently criticized. Partially in response to this criticism, Bernstein has gradually modified his claims, generally in the direction of a more complex (and less clear) correlation between socioeconomic class and the use of restricted and elaborated codes.

In his later work on codes, Bernstein qualifies the direct relationship between codes and class by stating, for instance, that working-class people may have "selective" access to elaborated codes. He also attempts to correct the lack of attention to the shaping force of context in his earlier formulation of the codes by proposing four "contexts" in which socialization occurs and in which a child learns restricted or elaborated codes: regulative, instructional, imaginative, and interpersonal. Finally, Bernstein very nearly abandons the relationship between class and language altogether by proposing that family types, "person-centred" or "positional," may affect the development of restricted or elaborated codes more than socioeconomic class. Positional families characteristically have clear and absolute relations of authority, "unambiguous definitions of status" (Bernstein, 1977, p. 184), while in "person-centered" families the "role system would be continuously evoking, accommodating, and assimilating the different interests and attributes of its members" (p. 185). The family types seem related to social class; many interpreters of Bernstein claim that "positional" families are working-class and "person-centered" families are characteristic of the middle class, but Bernstein himself is careful to only imply this relation: "These family types can be found empirically within each social class, although any one type may be rather more modal at any given historical period" (p. 184). The interesting feature of Bernstein's research is that in his search to find a correlation between class and language, he has found it necessary to nearly qualify the relationship out of existence.

Despite his reformulations, Bernstein's later theory is open to the same sort of critiques as his early theory. Michael Stubbs, for instance, in *Language, Schools and Classrooms* (1983), criticizes Bernstein for not basing his theory on actual observations of language use in context. He points out that there are no examples of real-life extended language use in any of Bernstein's papers. The lack of context-specific linguistic data leads to a serious critique: Even if one accepts that restricted and elaborated codes exist, Bernstein's assertion that these codes represent a speaker's understanding of "symbolic orders" remains open to question. The most common counterinterpretation, made by Labov and others, is that restricted and elaborated codes represent stylistic choices made by speakers in context, rather than intrinsic characteristics of their language. This reinterpretation has important consequences: in Bernstein's explanation "restricted codes" do indeed characterize working class language, and as such, lead to the conclusion that members of the working class use language in a less effective way than members of the middle class; working-class language, in this sense, is "deficient" compared to the norm of middle class language. The stylistic explanation does not see working-class language as deficient. Both elaborated and restricted codes are available to working-class and middle-class speakers, but the working-class speakers tend more frequently to choose restricted codes and middle-class speakers tend more frequently to choose elaborated codes. The stylistic explanation explains the linguistic variance as a matter of choice and perception of context, while Bernstein's theory explains the same variance as a feature of *ability*. Finally, Bernstein's theory has not been confirmed by any naturalistic studies, and indeed has been refuted by work by Labov (1972) and Ohmann (1982) (see below), so even the existence of elaborated and restricted codes, let alone Bernstein's explanation of them, is in question.[1]

Richard Ohmann, in "Reflections on Class and Language" (1982), articulates many of the above objections to Bernstein's work. In so doing, he outlines a relationship between class and language that recognizes speakers' ability, regardless of social background, to vary their speech according to their perception of the context. Ohmann objects to Bernstein on two central points. The first is that Bernstein's conception of language, or "code," is fixed, too inflexible to allow for what Ohmann calls one of "the cardinal principles of sociolinguistics," that speech is variable. The second objection has to do with Bernstein's conception of class. Ohmann argues persuasively that Bernstein assumes a definition of class that, like his understanding of language, is fixed and unchangeable. This definition of class is basically heuristic, arrived at by "calibrating one or more such factors as income, education, and occupation" (p. 8). Ohmann objects to this definition on roughly the same reasoning as Stubbs' objection to Bernstein's exploration of language: Bernstein's understanding of class "has no reality other than the heuristic one for the sociologist" (p. 9). Bernstein's conception of class has little relation to the actual experience of real people, just as his linguistic theories are unsupported by examples from actual language use.

Although Ohmann objects to Bernstein's conception of both class and language on empirical grounds, the strength of Ohmann's argument derives from the political motivation of his critique. The stable and static quality of Bernstein's definitions of class and language, especially when these stable and static conceptions define working-class language as deficient, work against teachers' and activists' efforts for a more egalitarian educational system and society. Ohmann argues, therefore, for conceptions of class and language that are contextual and dynamic, respectful of the minds and language of working-class people, and subject to human intervention. Ohmann defines class historically, differing significantly from Bernstein:

> I do not simply and eternally *belong* to the professional and intellectual portion of the working class. Rather in all my doing from day to day I and the people I mingle with and am affected by constantly *create* my class position. . . .

---

[1] See the postscript to Basil Bernstein (1977) for his claim that his concept of codes is not a deficit theory, especially pp. 250–253. He reacts specifically to Labov's statement in "The Logic of Non-standard English" (1972): "Bernstein's views are filtered through a strong bias against all forms of working-class behavior so that middle class language is seen as superior in every respect." Clearly Bernstein does not want his theory characterized as a deficit theory. Labov, however, is not alone. See Michael Stubbs, *Language, Schools and Classrooms*, 1983; Richard Ohmann, "Reflections on Class and Language," 1982, pp. 1–17; and Norbert Dittmar, 1976.

From this perspective, class is not a permanent fact, but something that continually *happens*. (p. 11)

Language, in Ohmann's definition of class, ceases to be only *reflective* of class, and becomes understandable in terms of *motive:* "My way of talking, whether 'caused' by my class or not, is one of the important means by which I, in my relations with other people, recreate my class, confirm it, perhaps alter it" (p. 11).

Ohmann's article owes some of its theoretical energy to Raymond Williams' excellent chapter on language in *Marxism and Literature* (Williams, 1977). Williams outlines a theory of language that is distinct from either a Saussurian arbitrariness or the kind of determinism that influences Bernstein's early work. Drawing on V. N. Volosinov's *Marxism and the Philosophy of Language* (1929), Williams argues that the relationship between sign and meaning, although conventional, is never arbitrary, as Saussure argued. It is instead "the result of a real process of social development, in the actual activities of speech and in the continuing development of a language" (p. 37).

The main force of Williams' argument, one relevant both to this chapter and to the book as a whole, it to conceive of language as "a social activity" and as "constitutive:"

> the real communicable 'products' which are usuable signs are . . . living evidence of a continuing social process, into which individuals are born and within which they are shaped, but to which they then also actively contribute. . . . (p. 37)

Like Ohmann, Williams argues against stable concepts of both language and society, stressing both process and variability. Unlike Bernstein's theories of codes, Williams, using Volosinov's term, argues for understanding language as "multi-accentual":

> [Language] must have an effective nucleus of meaning but in practice it has a variable range, corresponding to the endless variety of situations within which it is actively used. These situations include new and changing as well as recurrent relationships. . . . This variable quality, which Volosinov calls *multi-accentual,* is of course the necessary challenge to the idea of 'correct' or 'proper' meanings, which has been powerfully developed by orthodox philology from its studies of dead languages, and which had been taken over both into social-class distinctions of a 'standard' language flanked either by 'dialects' or by 'errors', and into literary theories of a 'correct' or 'objective' reading. (pp. 39–40)

These dynamic and context-specific definitions of class and language argue against a simple correlation between a social group and language features. There is no such thing as working-class language, identifiable by certain features such as reduced subordination or fewer abstractions. Instead, working-class people, like everyone else, use a variety of languages in a variety of contexts. Ohmann's and Williams' analyses suggest a relationship between class and language that doesn't aim for a direct correlation between class and language, and is therefore not open to the same criticisms as Bernstein's.

With this understanding of the relationship between language and class in mind, I would like now to turn to the examination of the work of Mr. C, beginning with his first essay, written in response to the question, "Write an essay telling the class who you are. Be as thorough as time allows."

> The question of "who a person is" has always been somewhat of a bother to me. Because outside of a facts list about a person, I feel this tends to place labels or stereotypes on a person. I personally always enjoyed the person, who, when asked this, commented—"I'm unique, exciting, and fantastic." I will attempt however, to label my self. I enjoy simple beauty, whether it be a person, thing or idea. I am a Christian, which I think is something very important. I am a family oriented person. I also am a firm believer in working up to your potential, or doing the best you can. There are a lot of things that I am, am not, or would like to be. It is a list far too long to mention in the time remaining. I guess to sum it up, I am me, and no one else but me.

In my experience, students commonly answer this question in three different ways. The first two are the most common, both "facts lists" of the type Mr. C rejects. First, a student will recite his or her geographical history, something like this: "I was born in Texas, and when I was six years old we moved to Connecticut. Then my dad got a job in Crawfordsville. This is my first year in college and I live in the dorms." In the second strategy a student will offer a list of hobbies, usually with an academic major thrown in: "Some of the things I like to do are water ski, aerobics, watch TV, jog, and major in Telecommunications." The third strategy is to reject the question, which is what Mr. C does in the first two sentences of his essay: "The question of 'who a person is' has always been somewhat of a bother to me. Because outside of a facts list about a person, I feel this tends to place labels or stereotypes on a person." Mr. C didn't stick with this strategy; perhaps he felt slightly uneasy about disobeying the question on the first day of class. After the sarcastic remark about the "unique, exciting and fantastic" strategy, Mr. C tries a facts list of his own: "I enjoy simple beauty, whether it be a person, thing or idea. I am a Christian, which I think is very important. I am a family oriented person. I also am a very firm believer in working up to your potential, or doing the best you can." Given that Mr. C admires a unique, exciting, and fantastic image, it is easy to understand why he didn't stick with the facts list. He wisely abandons it and again rejects the question, this time, more emphatically: "There are a lot of things that I am, am not, or would like to be. It is a list far too long to mention in the time remaining. I guess to sum it up, I am me, and no one else but me."

There are two themes in this first essay that remained important for Mr. C for the whole semester. The first is his reluctance to define himself in any concrete way; "who a person is" is a bother to him. Even his facts list is unusually abstract, general ideas and principles about very broad issues: beauty, Christianity, the family, and the work ethic.

The second theme I want to discuss may seem contradictory: At the same time Mr. C is refusing to define himself concretely, he is asserting himself as an individual. He reiterates the parodic, "I'm unique, exciting and fantastic," flamboyantly in his serious concluding phrase, "I am me, and no one else but me," and also by his wariness of stereotypes and labels. Perhaps both themes are embodied in the repetition of "person." The word is both an assertion of individuality as in "I personally always enjoyed. . . " and an abstraction, indicated by his repeated use of the indefinite article, "*a* person." In his one use of the definite article, "the person . . . who commented 'I'm unique, exciting, and fantastic,' " we have reason to doubt the actual existence of that person.

The first theme, that of resisting a concrete self-definition, became something of a moral stance for Mr. C. In an essay responding to Susan Glaspell's "A Jury of Her Peers" (1918), Mr. C identified with the sheriff's wife, Mrs. Peters, who, according to Mr. C, reserved her judgment, unlike everyone else in the story. He concludes that essay with the following moral: "Finally, too quick to judge is a big mistake. No one wins an election until all the votes are in, so wait until you have all the facts." While ostensibly a warning not to pass judgment too early, this conclusion recalls his objection to the facts list in essay 1. According to Mr. C, both the facts list about himself and the facts by which the characters in Glaspell's story judge innocence or guilt are incomplete and perhaps misleading. In the next essay, a personal experience essay about prejudice, Mr. C concludes: "People are people no matter what kind and there is good and bad in all of us." Again, note the reluctance to distinguish between people, to define and differentiate characteristics, and especially his refusal to pass judgment. All this in an essay about prejudice, a subject which usually invites differentiation between people and judgment of them.

A response statement to "Benito Cereno," Melville's (1967) tale of a slave mutiny, concluded a section of my course on ethnicity and language. Most students understood "language and ethnicity" to be the teacher's frame, and they construed "Benito Cereno" inside that frame. Mr. C rejected the frame, just as he rejected the question in essay 1. His conclusion will sound familiar: "Benito Cereno," he says, "serves as a reminder of how important it is not to come to conclusions based upon circumstantial evidence." This statement obviously correlates with his objection to the facts list and his statement that "too quick to judge is a big mistake" in the essay concerning "A Jury of Her Peers." All indicate his consistent reluctance to define himself and others concretely and separately.

These statements, and others like them, recurred enough in Mr. C's essays that Mr. C himself noted them in his analytical papers. In two of these analytical papers I required students to compare and contrast their language with the language of a fellow member of their small group. Mr. C fortunately had a group member with language habits that contrasted sharply with his own. His group member was prone to self-descriptions that were simple, direct, and clear, such as "I stink at science," or "I write a lot about sports because that's what I'm interested in." Perhaps this obvious contrast contributed to Mr. C's awareness of his reluctance to define himself simply and concretely. In his first analytical essay he states:

> [M]y essays seem to deal with abstract ideas. Things that could be taken in more than one context. I spoke of the sketchy concepts of identity in my first essay and describe feelings of ambivalence in my second.

In his next analytical paper, Mr. C noted an important contrast with his other group member, who tended to see gender and race in terms of obvious differences, and according to Mr. C, with "a sense of oppression." This contrast led Mr. C to the following insight about how he presented relationships in his essays:

> The relationships described within my writing were not good vs. bad or oppressor vs. oppressed rather they were not so clear cut. I expressed prejudice as a problem for everyone not just a chosen group of bad people . . . the lines [between these groups] were vague.

Keep in mind this first theme: the reluctance to draw distinct identities for people, to draw distinct "lines," especially the lines separating the social categories that I asked students to explore.

Now I am going to return to essay 1 and pick up the second theme, the theme of individuality, represented by Mr. C's parody of the wildly confident and showy person who said "I'm unique, exciting and fantastic,' " and his final statement, "I am me, and no one else but me." I have mentioned that in his response to "A Jury of Her Peers," Mr. C identified with Mrs. Peters because she "reserves judgment." Mr. C's based his identification on the fact that Mrs. Peters was the *only one* who reserved judgment. He refers to her as "the exception" and he uses that phrase three times in his essay. As in his response to "Benito Cereno," Mr. C does not construe the tale within the frame that I set up. We were, of course, discussing "gender and language." Mr. C did not interpret the story in terms of gender, but instead concentrated on the *individuality* of Mrs. Peters. I might add that in my experience with this story, identifying with Mrs. Peters is an exception in itself, for most students seem to identify with Mrs. Hale, the more talkative character.

Mr. C presents himself as "the exception" in a number of ways, but most importantly, he presents himself as the exceptional student. We get a glimpse of this in his first essay when he claims that one of the "facts" about himself is his belief in "working up to your potential, or doing the best you can." This theme is more pronounced in his response to Rebecca Harding Davis' *Life in the Iron Mills* (1972). Mr. C wrote this essay in response to the question.

> Read *Life in the Iron Mills.* After you are done, think over your reading experience and try to cite the moment when you experienced the strongest feelings, whatever they may be. Name and describe the feelings and cite the exact passage in the text. Then give an example of a time in your own history where you experienced similar feelings. Note that I am not asking you to name a time in your life when you were in the same situation as the one you cited in the book, just a time when you had the same feelings.

Here are excerpts from Mr. C's response:

> After reading *Life in the Iron Mills* by Rebecca Harding Davis, I was very depressed. . . . [T]he passage that evoked the most emotion . . . was the scene just after Hugh had seen his wife and was planning on killing himself. He had given up on everything in life and was determined on ending it. He was very cool and set in his task as if there was no alternative. He also came across like he didn't care even if there was an alternative.
>
> As I read this passage I felt myself fidgeting more than usual from my standard reading position. I felt helpless and very angry. I just wanted to grab him and say, "Fight! Life is too precious to throw away!" . . . I experienced similar feelings in talking to an old friend from high school some time back. She was ranked #1 in her class, but she was getting burned out on school. She also didn't want to be valedictorian. I found myself very frustrated in the same sort of way that I was in the book. I wanted to help her get over the rough times. I could not see, however, why she hadn't sought help and strength. I was mad, also that she didn't want to be valedictorian. I had been valedictorian of my graduating class. . .

This response shows several important features of Mr. C's self-presentation.

Most obvious is his seriousness about the value of education, which, by analogy, he equates with "life." He compares the frustration he feels toward Hugh for his suicidal feelings with the frustration he feels towards his friend who doesn't want to be valedictorian. His anger at her reveals the importance of that honor to him. The valedictorian, of course, is the exceptional student par excellence.

Mr. C frequently wrote about his experiences in high school. In his final paper, he describes high school life as a time when he was the exceptional student, the student that his teachers would turn to when no one else could answer the question. According to his report, his answer would always be met with, "that's exactly right." In this final paper, Mr. C finally chooses a label, a concrete self-definition: "The Perfect Student." He capitalizes it and puts it in quotation marks to call attention to its function as a label.

The Perfect Student, the *one* that teachers would turn to, these images of specialness in this second theme may seem to contrast with the first theme of refusing to distinguish himself and others. Mr. C, though, really only fails to define himself *socially*. If he did define himself socially, it would be at the expense of his exceptionality: To distinguish himself from one group would be to identify himself with another. Consider his remarks about gender: "I got no real feeling of gender my writing . . . no typically male stance." At the same time he is refusing to define himself socially by taking a "typical male stance," he is defining himself *individually* as an atypical male. This particular example serves both the theme of being exceptional, and also serves the theme of The Perfect Student, for in my course, I presented the topic of gender and language from a feminist point of view, and he most likely suspected that I would be supportive of an "atypical" male. Mr. C quite consciously wrote mainly for the teacher, and for the audience of this teacher he surely expected this solution to be met with, "that's exactly right."

The portion of my course that dealt with "class and language" was last of the three social categories. During this section, I noted changes in Mr. C's writing and in his behavior in the classroom. Up until this point in the semester, Mr. C had seriously written about very serious topics: the death of his brother, his failure to make his father proud, his mother's prejudice. In the eighth essay of ten, I asked the class to write about a time when something someone said to them made them realize a difference in class. This essay is his only humorous essay; it's about having to fill out the "dreaded FAF," the financial aid form. While he was filling out the form, his girlfriend called and he expressed his irritation with the form to her. Expecting to hear understanding sympathy, she instead said, "What's an FAF?" Mr. C had never before realized the families' financial differences before then, and he was shocked to understand that "she never had needed financial aid." In this essay, Mr. C does indeed recognize class differences, but the realization is, for all practical purposes, inconsequential. Mr. C concludes that he "was happy that she was spared the trouble" of filling out the form. The only apparent consequence of a class difference in Mr. C's essay is having to fill out a tedious form. Mr. C said as much in his analysis of this essay, "It was as if I was laughing it [the class difference] off, not taking the problem seriously."

At the same time Mr. C was writing in a more light-hearted vein, he seemed to be more frustrated, and slightly angry in person. He sat uncharacteristically silent and grim during class discussion. Up until the last few weeks, Mr. C had indeed maintained his status as The Perfect Student: perfect attendance, serious and punctual with his written work, a cooperative and sincere attitude. I suspect he wanted a grade, some indication that he was The Perfect Student in my eyes, but I don't give grades until the end of the semester. He also requested an extra conference in which he complained of not having anything to write about for his final retrospective essay.

In looking over Mr. C's essays, I see that the "frame" of class and language presented more problems for him than gender or ethnicity and language. I suspect that it was hard for him to ignore, and simultaneously more urgent and difficult for him to examine. He indicated the difficulty of this frame by saying in his third analytical paper that of all the subjects I asked him to write about, social class proved "to be the most difficult to reckon with." In the last essay, a response statement to Hemingway's "The Doctor and the Doctor's Wife" (1925), Mr. C uncharacteristically addressed differences in class:

> The fact that the author portrayed the wealthy man as one who would steal but had an uneasy conscious and the poor indian as one who would steal with a clear conscious upset me. This gives the impression that somehow a wealthy man is more moral than a poor one.

Sometime during these last weeks of my class Mr. C put it all together; he wrote a superb and surprising final paper. He focused on the importance of his working-class background in shaping his language use. Here are some samples of his observations:

> I come from a lower middle class home. My parents are blue collar workers and we have neither the money nor the connection to get ahead. We are just somewhere back in the pack.

> I found that throughout my writing, I gave myself the means of getting ahead by making everything equal. Once I was even, I could succeed by hard work and strive for the best.

> As I said before I grew up in a very self-conscious lower middle class family. My mother has always had this paranoia that people think they're

better than she. I have spent my life telling my mother that she's just as good as anyone else. I think that through the verbal repetition trying to convince my mother, I convinced myself. Also, there is my own sub-conscious fear of feeling lower than someone else. So . . . there has been a breakdown in my willingness to recognize differences in people.

With this equality of people in my own mind and my striving for perfection to show others my equality to them, I achieve the motivation for success.[2]

In these statements, Mr. C richly and complexly explains both themes: The unwillingness to recognize differences in people acts like a social defense mechanism. If Mr. C did recognize differences, if Mr. C did fully face the fact that his girlfriend's "money and connections" made more difference than having to fill out a form, then he would have to recognize his own social disadvantages. In my experience, students very rarely describe their family's economic position as "somewhere back in the pack." In our culture, the myth of the classless society so influences students that even students who clearly come from wealthy families claim the middle class as their background. Mr. C was bucking a cultural habit. The second theme is also explained by Mr. C's working-class background: if Mr. C defined himself as an *individual,* then "hard work" and "striving for perfection" are the only qualities he needed to "get ahead," and there would be no need for money or connections. Describing himself, picturing himself, in a sense *constructing* himself as an individual, gives Mr. C "equal opportunity," something he felt he wouldn't have if he conceived of himself as "working class." Both themes work to give Mr. C a sense of the possibility of success.

Mr. C's writing, like that of most students, is based on the motive for success in the classroom. At its most mundane level, success means getting an "A." At a more interesting level, one more appropriate to Mr. C's sincere and serious nature, success means trusting in the teacher's ability to set up a context in which he can learn what the teacher wants him to learn and then get an "A." Neither of these motives is uncommon. What Mr. C's exploration of the relationship between his class and his language use shows is that achieving success comes in different forms, and has different costs for different students.

Returning, once again, to Mr. C's two themes, I would like to explore

---

[2] Mr. C refers to his class membership in this citation as "lower middle class." In my experience all students initially refer to their backgrounds as middle class, even very wealthy students. Earlier Mr. C calls his parents "blue collar workers" and he sees his family as "somewhere back in the pack" economically. A definitive description of what constitutes working class is beyond the scope of this study. Whether defined broadly as Ohmann does, as one who "must sell his or her labor power in order to live, having no significant capital" (Ohmann, 1982; p. 9), or more specifically by income or occupation, Mr. C's background would apply to nearly anyone's definition.

the forms and the costs of Mr. C's success, looking first at his reluctance to define himself socially. Mr. C explains the motive for this theme when he says that in order to "get ahead," he first had to make "everything equal" by not recognizing differences in people. Specifically, Mr. C did not want to recognize his own working-class background, for fear that, in his own mind, this recognition would make him feel "lower" and thus inhibit his success, or that a public declaration of his class background would be a disadvantageous factor in others' judgment of him, particularly the teacher's judgment. Both of these explanations seem valid.

We have seen examples of Mr. C's concern for his audience's judgment in my discussion of the theme of resisting self-definition, especially his wariness of stereotypes and labels. In addition to the instances I've discussed, Mr. C frequently referred to "judgment" or "judging" in his earlier essays. The admirable quality he finds in Mrs. Peters, in "A Jury Of Her Peers" (Glaspell, 1918) (a story he said should be retitled "A Judgment of Her Peers"), is that "she reserved judgment." Likewise, the lesson in "Benito Cereno" (Melville, 1967) is not to "jump to conclusions based on circumstantial evidence." In the context of Mr. C's other work, it seems reasonable that Mr. C's reading indicates a worry about *my* judgment of him. These statements act as warnings against prejudgment on the basis of his class background. These repeated requests to hold off judgment until all the facts are in make more sense in the context of his admission of a "sub-conscious fear of feeling lower than someone else." Mr. C wanted to prevent a preconceived judgment, one that would assess only on the basis of background.

As the semester progressed, Mr. C became less concerned about my negative reaction, and in the final paper he focuses almost entirely on how his class background affected his own attitudes about success in school. We can see in his reflections on the relationship between his class background and language use in my course how Mr. C internalizes the conflict between his class background and the educational system's negative judgment of it. What is ostensibly a struggle to achieve legitimacy in the eyes of teachers is also a struggle within himself. For instance, when Mr. C speaks about spending his "life telling my mother that she's just as good as anyone else," he reflects that he was also trying to convince himself, for he also fights the "sub-conscious fear of feeling lower." He explains the strategy of his unwillingness to recognize class differences as a strategy designed to bolster his own feelings of authority and confidence: "With this equality of people *in my own mind. . .* I achieve the motivation for success" (my emphasis).

As I indicated at the beginning of this chapter, we can't see "not making class distinctions" or "presenting oneself as an individual" as intrinsic characteristics of working-class language correlating directly to Mr. C's working-class background; part of Mr. C's rhetorical strategies were to avoid working-class identification. But one cannot conclude therefore that a relationship between class and language does not exist. Instead, we need to conceive of all language, including the language that working-class students use, as "multi-accentual," and reconceive of speakers of that language as actively shaping it use. And we need to look at Mr. C's patterns of language use as rhetorical features in the double context of a college classroom and a class society. Mr. C's strategy of not making distinctions has to do with his own inner anxiety about recognizing the consequences of his own class background. The consequences, as he sees it, are the disadvantages of having neither money nor connections to get ahead, the disadvantages of not being equal. This understanding was not something conscious, at least not until the final paper; Mr. C admits he had "never really realized" his habit of not recognizing social distinctions before my class. The most serious consequence of the habit, in my view, is that Mr. C, in not recognizing social distinctions in others, also cannot recognize his own social background.

This means that not only does Mr. C separate himself from the experience of his own childhood, but he also separates himself from those who share his background: his family, his friends, his neighborhood. We can see in Mr. C's essays a variety of instances where Mr. C is either in conflict with his background or somehow differentiates himself from it. In his high school peer group, Mr. C played a "special" role:

> I was looked up to by both friends and faculty, I was the teacher's favorite because I was such a good student. To the students, I was the guy whom you went to for advice, or school problems, and you definitely didn't do bad things around because I was religious.

Mr. C gives us an example of this type of role in his essay about the friend who didn't want to be valedictorian. In none of his essays does he present himself as part of his peer group, one of several people; instead he is isolated in the special role of advisor, or superior.

A more important and painful example of Mr. C's separation from his background occurs in his essay 3. This essay compares his identification with Georgiana with Mr. C's experience trying to help his father:

> It was one of those weeks for my father where there was a million things that needed to be done and not time to do them . . . I was feeling rather useless. So, on Saturday, dad was fixing the car and I was determined to help. Reluctantly, he let me lend a hand by carrying him tools. . . .
>
> I wasn't very knowledgeable, though, on the workings of a car or the tools it took to fix them. My father asked for a certain tool (I don't remember which) and I gladly ran to get it. The tool I returned with was not what he had asked for. He looked down and told me that I knew better and to go

and get the right one. I was shattered by my failure. I wanted so much to make him proud.

Mr. C is not a student who has experienced failure on the academic level, yet one senses a conflict between the success of his academic experiences and his relations with family and peers. His dissociation from his background directly relates to his educational ambitions, which in turn relate to what sociologists call upward mobility. Mr. C's academic success is predicated on the difficult denial of his background. He has paid for his academic success— and his attempt to move upward in the socioeconomic ladder—with the absence of collegiality with peers, and with a strained relationship with his family.

When Mr. C states, "[w]e are just somewhere back in the pack," he suggests the motive for his second theme of individuality—and indicates the relationship between theme one and theme two. Mr. C conceives of society as made up of "the pack" and its implied opposite, individuals. Given the choice between membership in the pack, where he had to fight constantly the sense of feeling lower, and the individual, we can see why Mr. C chose the latter. Indeed, Mr. C's very presence in college indicates that he has chosen to be an individual, because his peers and his family did not attend college. We can see the class-specificity of this conception of social choices by comparing Mr. C's understanding of "the pack" with his middle-class subgroup member who said, "I am basically middle class, and as a result of this, I take a view in which I am the rule and not the exception." Unlike his classmate, Mr. C cannot define himself as the "rule" and still achieve success.

The explanation for Mr. C's language strategies of avoiding class or group identification and asserting exceptionality involves looking at why Mr. C constructs the social world in terms of "the pack" and "the exception." It involves the interaction of an educational system focused on "judgment" (remember Mr. C's repeated warnings against premature judgment), and the prerequisite for upwardly mobile working-class children: academic success. Richard Sennett and Jonathon Cobb have explored the relationship between education and economics in their book, *The Hidden Injuries of Class* (1973). Particularly useful for my analysis of Mr. C is their term, "the badge of ability." First of all, we can see in Mr. C's candid reflection on the difficulties of a working-class background, the need for him to be upwardly mobile— to defend against the sense of feeling lower. Sennett and Cobb have understood our educational system as based on a particular—and class-related— characterization of ability. Ability is unequally distributed in society; there is, in Sennett and Cobb's words, a "fixed, 'natural' allotment of ability; the people who stood out as individuals were 'naturally' unlike the mass at the center, either because they were very smart or very dumb" (p. 59). Sennett and Cobb see the ideal representation of this characterization of ability in the bell-shaped curve "discovered" by Binet and Simon in their intelligence testing. What began as an observation of intelligence test results became, in our educational system, an ideology, a general and accepted understanding of the stratification of ability, a stratification reproduced in the grading practices of most teachers. The "bell curve" of ability separates everyone into "the pack" and "the exceptions." We define successful students as exceptional and separate from the pack of average students. Such a conception of intelligence and ability is especially problematic for working-class students like Mr. C, because, as Sennett and Cobb show, they begin with a negative conception of themselves as "back in the pack." Paraphrasing an attitude toward ability like that of Mr. C's, Sennett and Cobb put the relationship between upward mobility and ability like this:

> That ability is the badge of individual worth, that calculations of ability create an image of a few individuals standing out from the mass, that to be individual by virtue of ability is to have the right to transcend one's social origins. (p. 62)

This analysis can help explain why—when pressed—Mr. C came up with the label, "The Perfect Student," instead of working within the social categories I had set up for students. By doing this, Mr. C retained his individuality, asserted his "badge of ability," and—since the course was designed for students to examine their social backgrounds—neatly erased his working-class background. I should note that Mr. C never denigrates his background. Instead, his background seems absent, ignored. Sennett and Cobb's exploration of the meaning of being "back in the pack" helps explain the absences of any reference to background in Mr. C's work:

> Average, adequate, ordinary: it is a language wherein personal recognition of the few is balanced by impersonal toleration of the many; it is a matter of good versus neutral. . . . The creation of badges of ability requires the mass to be invisible men. (pp. 67–68)

The difficulty for a working-class student like Mr. C is that, unlike the teacher or intelligence tester who chooses between those with ability and those without, his choices involve parts of himself: his perception of himself as one with ability, and his understanding of himself as located socially in the working class. Mr. C, by his presence in college and by the way he presented himself in my class, certainly has chosen to rise socially and in so doing has to part with defining himself in terms of his backgrounds. This parting has consequences that we shouldn't overlook.

Richard Hoggart, in *The Uses of Literacy* (1957), has characterized working-class students who, through educational success, rise socially, as Scholarship Boys. Hoggart's study took place in England where scholarship boys are selected and separated perhaps much more obviously than in the American system of education, yet much of what Hoggart describes seems related to Mr. C's presentation of himself in my course. Like Sennett and Cobb, Hoggart is concerned with the "hidden injuries" of the boy who, through his academic promise, rises socially. Hoggart claims, as Sennett and Cobb do, that in the process of upward mobility through education the scholarship boy chafes against his environment. Hoggart sees the Scholarship Boy as anxious and uprooted, living with "the kind of anxiety which seems most to afflict those in the working-classes who have been pulled away from their original culture." This anxiety results in him being "progressively cut off from the ordinary life of his group. He is marked out early. . . . [H]e has brains—a mark of pride and almost a brand" (pp. 241–242). Hoggart goes on to show how the Scholarship Boy's working environment itself contributes to his self-definition as separate from his working-class surroundings. "Marked" by parents and teachers, both of whom see him as one with brains, he soon is separated from his family and his peers by virtue of his ability. He accepts a definition of himself based on brains alone, realizing that "brains are the currency by which he has bought his way, and increasingly, brains seem to be the currency that tells" (pp. 242–243). With Mr. C, we can see that the definition of himself as The Perfect Student is his "currency" that fills the absence of "money and connections" in his family.

The Perfect Student, Mr. C's badge of ability, is, unlike real dollars, an unstable currency. Like "beauty" for Ms. M, the badge of ability depends on recognition by others, mainly teachers, for its value. Hoggart's statement that Scholarship Boys tend to make their "schoolmasters overimportant, since they are the cashiers in the new world of brain currency" (p. 243), points to the source of the instability of the currency, for working-class students' means of upward mobility depends heavily on their teachers' judgment. Mr. C's construction of the rhetorical situation in my classroom, his understanding of the audience as the teacher, and his self-definition as The Perfect Student grows out of this intuitive understanding of himself only in terms of individual ability, and his sense of the vulnerability of this definition. Mr. C's explanation of why high school experiences were the subject matter of the majority of his essays illustrates the instability of his definition of self:

> It was a big adjustment for me to get used to college, and I found that I wasn't going to be nearly as successful, at least by my own standards. So by talking about high school I keep alive that time when I was the "Perfect Student."

Mr. C revealed an exceptional awareness of the teacher's power to judge. We have seen this in his early focus on "judgment," but we can also see it in his desire to repeat the gratifying experience of hearing "that's exactly right," the approval of his teachers in high school: "Since I was writing to you, the teacher, I searched for the 'exactly right' answer." Even more telling, Mr. C accords me a great deal of power: "You, the teacher, are in control of what is good, bad or stupid. . . ." We can see in this picture why Mr. C was relatively unconcerned about the reception of his work by his fellow students. His unconcern for the judgment of his peers is both a social habit which has its roots in the "marking" of Mr. C as one with ability, and a conscious aim to insure the reproduction of his exceptionality by writing to the "cashier" of his value, the teacher.

Mr. C's "breakthrough" in his final paper—for it really did seem a sudden understanding—has to be seen in the context of a teacher-student relationship defined in this way. On one hand, Mr. C truly discovered a connection between his working-class background and his language use in my course, a connection which was difficult for him to see because of the social pressures *not* to see it. On the other hand, he made this discovery at the bidding of the teacher, a teacher who, in Mr. C's understanding of the role, had the power to decide what was "good, bad, or stupid," the power to reproduce Mr. C's sense of self as The Perfect Student, the power to help Mr. C achieve success and upward mobility. So while Mr. C's achievement was truly original and independently done, and his paper was one of the few instances where he could integrate his background with his intellectual achievement and academic ambitions, his achievement was also the result of the old story: complying with the teacher, the arbitrator of goods.

There's an obvious question that follows my exploration of Mr. C's language use in the class. Mr. C had already suppressed the negative effects of growing up in a working-class family, most likely with some pain. The uncovering of this background was also difficult for Mr. C; he said as much and I noticed as much. At the end of my course, in part, as I've said, to comply with the teacher's wishes, he had come to a fairly explicit understanding of how his class background affected his language use in my classroom. The question is, was this good? Would Mr. C be better off continuing to forget his class background? Does the recognition of the effects of his class background handicap his future performance in school? Would he be better off conceiving of himself as an "individual" and therefore "equal"? He felt, on some level, even in my class, that it he would be better off not to explore it, and in some pedagogical contexts, I am sure he would be right. There's no doubt that I encouraged him to explore it, and that my encouragement made him feel safe to disclose his background and its effects. There's also no doubt that, early in the course, he refrained from disclosing his class background for good reasons, the reasons explored by

Sennett and Cobb, Hoggart and others, the fact that for many teachers, a working-class background remains at best irrelevant, at worst, a disadvantage.

To see the knowledge that Mr. C achieved during my course as somehow damaging seriously underestimates Mr. C and students with similar backgrounds. Mr. C's cautiousness concerning his background indicates his knowledge of the educational context. I don't believe that there is any danger that the process of learning that Mr. C went through in my class will have any deleterious effects on his educational success. Mr. C will continue to achieve cautiously, but now with increased consciousness of the form of his achievement and the costs.

Mr. C's increased consciousness about the relation between his working-class background and his language use in my course has some clear affirmative features. Unlike his prior educational experience, he found a way in my course to see his working-class background as a source for academic achievement. In fact, it was *only* through his candid exploration of his background that he could explain his language use complexly. This is not usually the case. As Hoggart, Sennett and Cobb and others have shown, academic success depends on breaking these important and potentially enriching class bonds.

Mr. C's evaluation of his language, his characterization of it early in the semester as "complex," "abstract," "inquisitive" and so on, indicated that he felt his language was appropriate for academic success (note that Mr. C defines his language similarly to Bernstein's "elaborated codes"). To connect the development of awareness of language use in my classroom with what he felt initially was a handicap, his working-class background, is to make a connection that makes possible an integration of his desire for academic success and his background. Mr. C's exploration of his background also led to him to see how class exists for him on a concrete, experiential level, and that it mattered—even in everyday interactions in the classroom. Though perhaps rudimentary, this is the kind of class-consciousness that makes for a critical understanding of oneself and one's world.

5
Writing is Like an Enemy: Schooling and the Language of a Black Student

Mr. C's experience as a working-class student has much in common with the experience of the student whose work I examine in this chapter. Both students considered their backgrounds liabilities in the foreign world of higher education; both students had little or no confidence that they could tap the rich experiences of their background to help them succeed in college; and both students attempted to minimize the influence of their backgrounds on the way they used language in the classroom. For Ms. N, my example in this chapter, the attempt to make her background fade harmlessly away proved more difficult than for Mr. C. Ms. N was one of two black students in a classroom of 25 students. Although she had full command of Standard English, her spoken dialect—the perception of which was shaped by students' and teacher's simultaneous knowledge of her skin color—"marked" her in a way Mr. C never was or could be. Mr. C saw class boundaries as flexible, in part due to his ability to be academically successful, to masquerade as a middle-class student until he had actually achieved a socially favorable position. Ms. N faced many of the same barriers as Mr. C, but Ms. N couldn't "pass" or masquerade in the way that Mr. C could. Ms. N's use of the conventions of Standard English and academic prose suggest, perhaps, a similar strategy of playing along, but I have no doubt that the barriers confronting Ms. N were greater and more difficult to overcome than those confronting Mr. C. There were other differences as well. Ms. N began my course clearly aware of a conflict between the social and educational demands made on her to use Standard English, spoken and written, and her own love for and use of street language. This conflict translates into a social one between her wish for assimilation and success in the dominant culture by adopting Standard English, and a desire to differentiate herself by embracing the cultural habits and traditions of her own social group, including using what she called street language. Her awareness of this conflict, gained through educational experiences, led her to adopt a much more skeptical attitude towards my course than Mr. C.

The purpose for my exploration of Ms. N's attitudes and their effect on her language use in my classroom contributes to the concern of my book as a whole: the exploration of how students' memberships in social groups influence their language use in the classroom and an argument for a pedagogy that will work against sense of exclusion that many working-class, black, and women students feel in education. I focus, in this chapter, on the consequences for Ms. N of the social stratification of races. I understand Ms. N's language use in a double context, similar to the ones in Chapters Three and Four: (a) a society that stratifies wealth, prestige, and opportunity on the basis of race, and (b) a classroom where Ms. N was one of two black students in a course taught by a white teacher. The course was a section of the regular freshman English requirement, neither the advanced sequence nor the basic one. Given this context, I obviously do not seek to make generalizations about "Black English" in any general sense, but instead I explore a black student's use of language in this particular setting.

Perhaps this setting may strike readers as an especially limited and limiting one to understand the language of black students. And in part, I agree. Indeed, I argue implicitly in my case study that an all-white or nearly all-white classroom presents immense disadvantages for understanding the connection between social relations between races and language use, a disadvantage for white students and white teachers, as well as for black students and teachers. Understanding one's own perspective demands the presence of other, differing perspectives. So while I have been all along arguing for changed goals for reading and writing instruction, I also wish to argue for a changed student body and faculty in order achieve these goals. My aim that students achieve a sense of self-consciousness and responsibility in their language use rests upon understanding diverse uses of language. The resources for such an understanding in an all-white classroom are obviously limited. At the same time I advocate the necessity of having greater numbers of minority students and teachers in the language classroom, the context of a classroom with two or three minority group members may in fact be, at present, a useful context for many teachers, for outside of inner-city universities or all-black universities this situation represents the norm and thus offers an appropriate research context.

An understanding of how race affects language use entails examining the teaching of Standard English in the classroom. In the 1960s, the theoretical justification for teaching Standard English to black students grew from the deficit theories of working-class language that I discussed in the opening pages of the last chapter, particularly Bernstein (1977). Researchers drew upon Bernstein's early work on codes to justify their program for redressing what they saw as the inadequate language skills of black children. These researchers understood black children's difficulties in school as the result of the lack of exposure to language, as "linguistic deprivation." The classic refutation of this argument is William Labov's "The Logic of Non-standard English" (1972), which not only demonstrates the equality of working-class or black language, but suggests the superiority of black dialect over middle-class language. Labov's conclusion is unequivocal:

> The concept of verbal deprivation has no basis in social reality. In fact, black children in the urban ghettos receive a great deal of verbal stimulation, hear more well-formed sentences than middle-class children, and participate fully in a highly verbal culture. (p. 201)

Labov sees the myth of verbal deprivation as "particularly dangerous, because it diverts attention from real defects of our educational system to imaginary defects of the child" (p. 202). He notes that the deficit theorists failed to see black language in any relevant social context. Instead, researchers typically interviewed the child about language patterns in the home and generally neglected direct observation of the home life itself.[1] Labov's work shows how the context of a research interview between a white researcher and a black child produces "deprived" responses of silence, monosyllabic replies, and avoidance because of the asymmetry of privilege in the interview. He cites a similar case of a "deprived" response in his own research, and then goes on to show with the same informant that changing the research context to one where the child feels more natural produces language displaying a "rich array of grammatical devices" (p. 212). Labov's conclusion supports my emphasis on context: "[that] the social situation is the powerful determinant of verbal behavior and that an adult must enter into the right social relation with a child if he wants to find out what a child can do" (p. 212).

Labov's article has been widely influential and most researchers no longer accept the verbal deprivation theory. Recently, however, the theory has been revived in changed terms by researchers in orality and literacy. Walter Ong, in *Orality and Literacy* (1982) and "Literacy and Orality in Our Times" (1977), makes the analogy between black urban speakers and primary oral cultures; he sees in urban black culture a "heavy oral residue." Although Ong frequently credits oral cultures for various reasons, he sees residually oral cultures as linguistically deficient, and he privileges literate culture. When Ong attempts to present oral cultures as equal he nearly always qualifies his statements, as in, "Of course oral cultures do not lack originality of their own kind," or "Oral thinking, however, can be quite sophisticated

---

[1] Two commonly cited examples are Martin Deutsch and associates, *The Disadvantaged Child* (1967), and Carl Bereiter and Siegfried Englemann, *Teaching Disadvantaged Children in the Preschool* (1966). Labov's own work using black interviewers is discussed in *Language in the Inner City* (1972), pp. 205–212.

and in its own way reflective" (Ong, 1982, p. 41, p. 57) The qualifiers, "of their own kind" and "in its is own way" indicate Ong's refusal to grant equal value to oral cultures. When he applies these findings to people inhabiting "residually oral" cultures, such as urban blacks, one can see the "residue" of deficit theory. In "Literacy and Orality in Our Times," Ong makes the claim that urban black culture is "basically a primary oral culture." The consequences, according to Ong, are that black urban students are incapable of analyzing their world: "In a primary oral culture, intensive analysis is not practiced, not even thought of." In *Orality and Literacy,* Ong's statements about primary oral culture are even more damning: Oral cultures are not only not analytical, they are not objective, not as original, not as creative, not interested in definitions, not dynamic, unable to delineate finer shades of meaning or degree, and so on (Ong, 1982, pp. 37–57).

The most troublesome aspect of Ong's work is his certainty that writing restructures consciousness in a predictable and valuable way. Ong makes this point over and over in *Orality and Literacy:*

Writing . . . restructures thought. (pp. 7–8)

In an oral culture, restriction of words to sound determines not only modes of expression but also thought processes. (p. 33)

More than any other single invention, writing has transformed human consciousness. (p. 78)

Writing heightens consciousness. (p. 82)

So not only does Ong see oral culture as linguistically deficient, but because of his certainty of the relationship between literacy and cognitive ability, oral cultures are deficient cognitively as well.

Ong takes care not to state his case as baldly as I have just done; he repeatedly assures the reader that oral cultures are just as good as literate ones. But this train of thought is clear and if Ong aims for fair-mindedness, one of his students, Thomas Farrell, is not so cautious. Farrell recently published "IQ and Standard English" (1983). I cite it not so much because of its influence (articulate responses by Karen Greenberg (1984), Patrick Hartwell (1984), Margaret Himley (1984), and R. E. Stratton (1984) should limit its influence), but because Farrell's work demonstrates the negative consequences of Ong's thought.

Farrell attempts to suggest a program for remediating the low IQ scores of black urban children. Citing Ong (1977), he notes that black urban children inhabit a residual form of a primary oral culture. Noting the persistently low IQ scores of urban black students, Farrell concludes that a "primary oral culture" *causes* the low IQ scores by black children, based on his certain knowledge that "literacy does indeed bring about some of the mental developments measured by IQ tests" (p. 476). Like Ong, he assumes the inability of members of oral cultures to think abstractly. Farrell then assumes that oral language itself causes low IQ scores, and searches for formal features in Black English that would be the source of the defect in thinking. He focuses, not surprisingly, on the most well-known feature of Black English Vernacular, the deletion of the copula: "the non-standard forms of the verb 'to be' in various regional forms of Black English may affect the thinking of the users" (p. 477). I don't want to go into the arguments against Farrell; his critics easily refute him.[2] My point is that his thinking, however wrong, was made possible by two of Ong's assumptions: (a) that oral and written cultures are fundamentally different and distinct and (b) this difference is not only linguistic, but cognitive, too.[3]

Much recent research suggests that Ong overstates the differences between oral and literate forms. Mary Louise Pratt, using Labov's analysis of "natural" (oral) narratives, shows how all storytelling, oral or written, follows essentially the same formula. Pratt (1977) and Labov (1972) contend that narratives, written and oral, begin with an abstract, are then followed by an orientation, a complicating action, an evaluation, a result or resolution, and then a coda. Note that this formula itself, originally arrived at by Labov in his analysis of oral narratives by Harlem residents, argues against many of the traditional characteristics assigned to orality. Ong (1982) claims that oral language use is "additive," but Labov's examples show that these narratives do not string together bits of information: They develop, build, and resolve. Many researchers also claim that oral language depends on a shared, but unstated context, and that oral cultures are unable to "decontextualize" language.[4]

---

[2] The responses by Greenberg (1984) and Hartwell (1984) are particularly germane. Greenberg, for instance, also sees Farrell's work in the context of deficit theory:

> Given the ways in which America's sociopolitical climate has changed in the past decade, we should have expected that someone was bound to come along and argue, once again, that the inferior performances of black children on IQ tests is due to deficits in the children rather to defects in our social and educational systems. (p. 455)

Hartwell shows conclusively how the deletion of the copula is irrelevant to the question of analytical thinking: "Russian and Hebrew, to cite common examples, lack a form equivalent to English *to be,* and this does not seem to have diminished the cognitive capacity of, say Vygotsky or Luria" (p. 463). Hartwell shows that Farrell is not only racist, but ethnocentric as well.

[3] Geneva Smitherman-Donalson makes a similar argument in "Discriminatory Discourse on Afro-American Speech" (1988). Concluding her discussion of Farrell's "IQ and Standard English," Smitherman-Donalson states: "Once again, the differences are not simply differences, but as in the racist scholarship of the past, the differences amount to deficits" (p. 166).

[4] Many researchers have claimed that writing requires "decontextualization." In practice, this means that writers must provide the context in language rather than assume it. Some researchers in orality and literacy claim that people from oral cultures, because they do not write, cannot "decontextualize." See Cook-Gumperz and Gumperz, "From Oral to Written: The

The narratives that Labov cites do not assume a context; the purpose of the orientation is essentially to set the context, in Labov's words: "to identify in some way the time, place, persons and their activity or the situation" (p. 364). In addition, these narrative structures reveal analytic and abstract thought. Occasionally the coda and usually the abstract function as conclusions or summaries, neither of which could exist without analytic thought. Pratt goes on to use these categories, derived from an oral culture, to explain the structure of literary works, concluding that literary works and natural narratives are "utterances of the same type" (p. 69).

If Pratt's work shows the "oral" in the "literate," Deborah Tannen's (1982) work shows the "literate" in the "oral." Tannen has done most of her work analyzing actual conversions, analyses that dispell easy distinctions between oral and written language use. In her studies comparing Greek and American language use, Tannen notes that Greek speakers typically rely on "oral" conventions; they show a fondness for the oral convention of formulaic phrases (such as cliches) and for personal or subjective responses to situations. Americans, on the other hand, seem uncomfortable with cliches, and frequently apologize for using them. In addition, they tend to objectify their responses to situations, a practice Tannen associates with written culture. If we accept Ong's thesis that literacy changes cognitive structures, then one would assume that the Greeks were from an oral culture, but of course, both Greek and American cultures are highly literate ones. Tannen explains that the differences in Greek and American language use originate in social values rather than intellectual or linguistic abilities; she concludes:

> matters are more complex than had been thought. It will not do to label some people as oral and others as literate. Individuals and groups can make use of strategies that build on interpersonal involvement and make maximal use of paralinguistic and prosodic channels that are lost in writing; or strategies that focus on content and make maximal use of lexicalization, as these serve their context-bound needs and as these have been conventionalized in their speech habits. (1982, pp. 13–14)

Both the strategies of communication in oral cultures (such as "interpersonal involvement") and strategies of communication available to literate cultures (such as "focus on content") depend less on "oral" or "written" capabilities than on the speaker's situation and ethnic and social background.

Shirley Brice Heath's (1982, 1983) work, already referred to in Chapter Two, supports Tannen's conclusions. Her detailed work with residents of

---

Transition to Literacy" (1981). As an aside, Gumperz' own work in conversational analysis shows that oral language use demands setting and negotiating the context and suggests that contextualization is done in all language situations. See Chapter Six of *Discourse Strategies* (Gumperz, 1982).

Trackton, the black, supposedly "oral" community, revealed a multitude of uses for writing and leads her to conclude:

> the traditional distinctions between the habits of those characterized as having either oral or literate traditions may not actually exist in many communities of the United States which are neither non-literate or fully literate. (1982, p. 94)

Like Tannen, Heath finds a detailed cultural examination of the uses of literacy more useful than the summary of abstract qualities of oral or written cultures:

> descriptions of the concrete context of written communication which give attention to social and cultural features of the community as well as to the oral language surrounding written communications may discredit any reliance on characterizing particular communities as having reached either restricted or full development of literacy or as having language forms and functions associated more with the literate tradition than with the oral, or vice-versa. (p. 94)

Like Heath, Sylvia Scribner and Michael Cole (1978) have found that detailed analysis of literacy practices in a social or cultural context makes generalizations about literacy, such as those made by Ong and Farrell, difficult to make. Scribner and Cole did field work among the Vai in West Africa. The fact that the Vai invented a writing system that is integrated in their daily life and taught outside of institutional structures made this cultural context specifically important:

> their writing and reading are not activities separate from other daily pursuits, nor does learning to read and write require a person to master a large body of knowledge that is unavailable from oral sources. (p. 453)

What makes this cultural context especially interesting is that it enables Scribner and Cole to study the effects of literacy separate from the effects of schooling. When separated from schooling, Scribner and Cole found that the development of literacy *had no effect* on cognitive abilities:

> Vai literates were not significantly different from nonliterates on any of these cognitive measures, including the sorting and reasoning tasks that had been suggested as especially sensitive to experience with a written language. (p. 453)

After discovering these findings on the basis of surveys and standardized tests, Scribner and Cole turned to ethnographic methods resembling Heath's

work in *Ways With Words.* In exploring and describing the various habits
of literacy with the Vai, Scribner and Cole found that literacy skills did
have psychological consequences, but these consequences are "highly specific
to activities with the Vai script," that is, culturally and situationally specific:
"restricted—perhaps to the practice actually engaged in or generalized only
to closely related practices" (p. 457). Scribner and Cole's research argues
exactly against the type of generalizations that Ong and Farrell make: "We
did not find that literacy in the Vai script was associated in any way with
generalized competencies such as abstraction, verbal reasoning, or metalin-
guistic skills" (p. 457).

These studies by Scribner and Cole, Tannen, and Heath suggest a more
flexible and tolerant understanding of literacy and orality than Ong's or
Farrell's. Taken together, they forcefully argue for the role that social
context plays in shaping both actual language practices and cognitive abilities.
For a deficit model to work, it needs both a clear distinction between oral
and literate language use and the assertion that this distinction has serious
consequences, neither of which is supported by Scribner and Cole, Heath,
or Tannen. Tannen asserts that speakers' choice of either oral or written
strategies depends on the immediate conversational context and the social
and ethnic backgrounds of the participants. Heath makes the point that
once one understands a community's language use *in detail,* the usefulness
of the distinction between oral and literate dwindles, because in our culture
they have "protean shapes" (p. 116). Her work argues against Ong's and
Farrell's contention that there could exist a "primary oral culture" in
American society and against the usefulness of the distinction at all. Heath's
work with a black community, one which Ong and Farrell would label
"oral," makes her case particularly strong. Scribner and Cole's argument
that literacy does not necessarily produce general cognitive consequences
suggests that instead of privileging one kind of language activity, a particular
kind of writing to "heighten consciousness," literacy teaching be tailored
to the needs and goals of specific cultures or subcultures. Restricted senses
of orality and literacy can turn a "difference" into a "deficit," not only a
linguistic deficit, but a cognitive one, as Ong and Farrell demonstrate.

Geneva Smitherman (1977) puts this issue into a political context in her
discussion of models of "difference" in *Talkin and Testifyin.* She notes, as
my discussion of orality and literacy shows, how easily "difference in kind"
theorists turn into "difference in value" theorists. The transformation is
made possible by the fact that researchers who advocate such models, such
as Ong or Farrell, extract language use from a shaping social and political
context:

> Like deficit theorists, bi-dialectal theorists ["different but equal" theorists]
> either ignore or incorrectly conceptualize the interaction between language,

school, and the larger political reality. Schools, curricula, language teaching policies, and classroom practices are not autonomous entities, nor do they exist in a sociocultural vacuum. Rather, they are interrelated with and governed by the pervasive political and economic ideology of America. Talking about Black English, listing its features and suggesting ways of changing or adding to it, without commensurately advocating changes in the sociopolitical system in which black people struggle is not only short-sighted, it amounts to so much pure academic talk, and ultimately, is an implicit acknowledgement that the system is good and valid, and all that need be done is to alter the people to fit into it. (p. 207)

The history of bidialectalism is an extremely complex one, beyond the scope of this study.[5] I cite Smitherman because she so clearly understands language use and language instruction in a social and political context. Any proposed change in language use for the purposes of improving the lives of black people must be accompanied by a concurrent social and political change. She argues that without social and political change, changing black language use amounts to a coercive insistence on conformity. Smitherman articulates a sense of language that has relevance to the use of language by black students in my course, one that respects the linguistic and cognitive capabilities of minority students, one that does not rely on restricted senses "difference," such as definitions of orality and literacy. As with the discussion of language use by women in Chapter Three, and working-class language in Chapter Four, Smitherman's understanding of black language use recognizes the speakers' active and flexible ability to vary his or her style. Speakers of black English speak in contexts: socioeconomic and historical ones and specific, day-to-day contexts. Like all language users, they can choose from a range of stylistic options that adapt to changing language situations. These choices, though, also reflect historical habits. Smitherman notes that even when the situational context may suggest that a speaker will use Standard English—in school, for instance—a speaker may choose to retain features of Black English Vernacular to demonstrate affinities with the black community (p. 12).

The ability to speak both Standard English and Black English Vernacular creates what Smitherman calls "linguistic ambivalence" (p. 174), that is, a conflict between wanting to "git ovuh" (succeed) in American society and

---

[5] I have chosen to focus on orality and literacy in this chapter because issues similar to those of bidialectalism have recently been raised in these terms. For statements on bidialectalism, see James Sledd, "Bi-dialectalism: The Linguistics of White Supremacy" (1969); Wayne O'Neil, "The Politics of Bidialectalism" (1971). More recently the issue has been revived by an unsuccessful effort to revise the Conference on College Composition and Communication's resolution, "The Students' Right to Their Own Language" (1974). See Sledd, "In Defense of *The Students' Right*" (1984); and Thomas Farrell and James Sledd, "Comment and Response" (1984).

therefore speak Standard English and wishing to retain the strong and enriching cultural, historical, and linguistic features of black language. Gumperz, in "Interactional Sociolinguistics in the Study of Schooling" (1986), also notes the range of styles available to black speakers and notes a similar ambivalence in the use of these styles. Like Smitherman, John J. Gumperz connects stylistic choice with a social and political context:

> On one hand, the need for communication at work and in other public settings has brought about significant adaptations to the majority speech, so that many speakers are now bidialectal, that is they control a range of styles and dialects which vary from forms which are quite close to Standard English to more traditional Black English forms. On the other hand, however, intergroup contact itself, and the relationship to power differential and domination associated with it, tend to act as a counterforce to prevent complete linguistic assimilation. (p. 50)

These characterizations of black language use by linguists such as Smitherman, Gumperz, Heath, and Labov argue against a simplistic characterization and classification of black language as "oral" and certainly against any deprivation or deficit model. In its place we have active language users, embedded in social and cultural history, with a variety of stylistic choices at their disposal, who change their language according to their perception of the specific context.

Using the double context of the specific classroom and a larger social context of a social structure where privilege and opportunity is stratified according to race, the following analysis of a black student's language use explores how students and teachers resist and reproduce contemporary race relations, race relations involving contradictory forces towards assimilation and differentiation. I begin my analysis by stating that "race" or race relations as explicit issues are completely absent from Ms. N's "public" essays, the essays that had the potential of being duplicated for the class as a whole. In her analytical papers, although she still doesn't explicitly mention race relations as a topic, she does talk about growing up in "the ghetto," being "bussed out," and frequently mentions high- and low-class environments, which correspond to "white" and "black" respectively. She had an obvious reason for not making race an issue in her public essays: Her fear of a negative reaction from the 23 white classmates. She had good reason for this fear. I separate students into small groups alphabetically on the basis of their last name. It so happened that Ms. N and the one other black student had last names beginning with the same letter and so were grouped together with a white male. The white student came up to me after he found out about the grouping and requested to be moved to another group. He responded to my irritated "why?" by stating he didn't think he could contribute much to their education because he wasn't "used to" black people. Such attitudes make Ms. N's reluctance to introduce racial issues in her essays understandable.

More than for most students, the history of Ms. N's experience in other English classes shaped our relationship. I knew from the first week that she had not done well in an earlier attempt to pass freshman English and had dropped the course because of a failing grade. Something of her experience failing this earlier English class may have influenced her first essay, for she begins with "The most important aspect in my life is the way I deal with complicated and depressing situations." No doubt failing her English class was complicated and depressing and no doubt that the comment that follows, her statement that she likes "a good challenge," reflects her desire to communicate to me her earnestness in taking the course over.

The failure in her earlier attempt at freshman English was not her only bad experience with English courses. In fact, several reported experiences with English teachers amounted to something of a theme for Ms. N. The following story is representative:

> In the past I felt very uncomfortable in my English classes, I always felt that the teacher would criticize everything I said if I talked the way that I'm use to. Once I was in this English class and the teacher was a real critic, every thing you did was wrong. One day she called on me to go in front of the class and speak. I felt that she was picking on me cause I never did say much in the class room. She started asking me a lot of question using a lot of big words. I think she thought I was not going to respond and when I did she looked very surprise, because I set up front of the room putting on a big front. I talked so proper and pronouncing every syllable. I do admit I was very nervous but handle the situation very calmly.

Note that Ms. N presents this as a success story, a time when she triumphed over "the real critic." In the understandable way that Ms. N conceived of her choices in this situation, she could either endure criticism by talking the way she's used to, or she could, with anger and resistance, show the teacher that even though she doesn't want to "talk proper," she has the ability, if she so chooses, to do so. Ms. N's vilification of her former English teacher, just or unjust, serves an important rhetorical purpose as a message to me saying, "don't you treat me this way." Yet despite my intention not to behave like "a real critic," despite my repeated statements defining the purposes of the course as "understanding" and "responsibility" instead of correct English, Ms. N continued to limit herself to the choice of "enduring criticism" or "with anger and resistance" complying with the teacher's wishes for Standard English. Enduring criticism, choice number one, apparently, was the worse of the two. In one essay, a response statement to Hemingway's "The Doctor and the Doctor's Wife" (1925), Ms. N compared the fight between Doc and Dick to a serious conflict she experienced with her best friend. The source of the conflict, according to Ms. N, was her friend's habit of "correcting every thing [Ms. N] did." Additionally, in reference to my course, she frequently mentioned her relief at not having to "worry about anyone criticizing the way I speak." In an essay where she was asked to describe my language, she translated "language" to "teaching" and commented:

> One feature I think about your method of teaching is, I like how you sit down and think what was this person thinking about and why did she (or he) write this. It gives a student a more positive image of himself for a teacher to sit with him and discuss his paper with him rather than to throw the paper back with a whole lot of negative remarks on how the person writes. I was surprise when I got my paper back. I was use to a teacher pointing out the negative part of my paper. But pointing out the positive things is a lifter to the student. I think your method of teaching is good so far I hope it stay that way.

The last comment, "I hope it stay that way," goes a long way towards explaining this whole essay. Above all, Ms. N is asking me not to start pointing out negative features of her language. Additionally and importantly, she also expresses her suspicions; My method is good "so far." As far as I can tell, nothing I did (or perhaps could do) ever really dispelled her doubts; she always wondered if I would begin criticizing and correcting her language.

Ms. N's doubts about my sincerity have their roots in her past experiences in English classes. We have seen already Ms. N's presentation of an English teacher's usual behavior; an English teacher "criticizes," "corrects," and "picks on her." Understanding this antagonistic relationship between Ms. N and English teachers necessitates examining how bad experiences in English classes like the one Ms. N talks about above relate to her complicated and thorough understanding of the relationship between social group and language, an understanding that existed before my course. In a paper where she was asked to explore how a "community" of the student's choice affected his or her language use, Ms. N discussed the complex relationship between "street language" and the language of a "middle- to high-class person:"

> When I go different places I find myself talking differently than I would if I was with my regular gang. Sometimes I feel that it is appropriate to change the way you use your language, especially when you are in a totally different environment. This does not mean that you are being a phony, it is just that you should speak the language that they are use to hearing. For example, in

a lower to middle class neighborhood the language is very cool and straight out of the street. They uses phrases such as: "I'm hip," "You're a trip," "Bug that," "Don't do me," etc. These phrases are used to be cool or just to fit in with the rest of the group. Say for instance you were in a home of a fairly rich person, you would not use that language in their present. Your conversation would be totally different. When we got around someone who was from a higher class environment, we would start speaking as if we were English majors.

Ms. N first of all demonstrates one of the basic facts of language that I have been presenting in this study, that language is motivated by social context, frequently involving stratified relationships between social groups. Ms. N's description of her language use bears a resemblance to the sociolinguistic concept of situational code switching. As Gumperz (1982) defines it, situational code switching refers to the alteration of language (in bilingual speakers), or dialect (in bidialectal speakers), according to a setting (home, school, work, etc.), or an activity (formal speaking, special ceremonies, games, etc.), or a category of audience (friends, family, strangers, social inferiors, government officials, etc.) (1982, p. 60). In the cases referred to by Ms. N, she alters her language according to socioeconomic class environment. Though she doesn't explicitly state that these environments are "racial" as well as "socioeconomic," I have no doubt that in practice they are. Note particularly that she identifies "talking like an English major" with the social context of a "high class environment," associating English with both "upper class" and implicitly "white."

Sociolinguistic analyses of code switching, such as Gumperz's, usually exclude a sense of affect associated with alternating codes. Ms. N's analyses, however, show that the feelings experienced in conversations between differing social groups often motivates the change in speech style. For instance, Ms. N frequently seems to feel coerced into changing her speech style. This sense of coercion isn't immediately apparent in the above citation. She seems entirely able and willing to change her language for a "fairly rich person." She does not consider this being a "phony," although her denial indicates that she has considered the possibility. She sums up her sense of these language issues with what appears as an easy relativism, "you should speak the language that they are used to hearing," or rephrased in the next paragraph, "I feel it would be proper to speak in the same manner as the person you are talking to." Ms. N's idea of rhetoric reflects Ms. M's in Chapter Three, that one should change one's language to fit the "comfort" of the audience. The difference is that for Ms. N, the language change is even greater and signals a more obvious social difference. Ms. M, as I explained in Chapter Three, changed her subject matter and her degree of disclosure because of a fear of rejection. Ms. N changes her language because of a certainty that teachers, classmates, and others will recognize a language "straight out of the street." And certainly, in her mind, this recognition will entail the penalties of "correction" and "criticism" from teachers. And from students? The penalties are just as stiff:

> [Changing one's language] is all done to show others whether they are from a high class environment or a low one, it shows them that you can relate to them even though you may have a different background. We were taught a big lesson on that when we were bussed out. If you did not talk as if you knew good grammar you would personally get turned out.

I did not inform Ms. N of her white subgroup member's desire to change small groups, but his response to participating in a small group with her is surely an example of getting "turned out." Getting turned out, criticized, and corrected are the "penalties" for not speaking Standard English. Linguists like Labov have demonstrated over and over that no linguistic reason exists for these penalties, that Black English Vernacular is as systematic, as suited for successful communication as Standard English. The penalties are therefore socially and racially motivated, as Ms. N clearly indicated by placement of language change within the context of school bussing and high and low classes. Is it any wonder that Ms. N isn't usually comfortable in English classes? Her understanding of language shows how theories of "difference" get changed into theories of "deficit," for in her presentation of language differences, look who's having to do make all the adjustments, look who's changing for whom. Ms. N's description of situational code switching indicates that she is the one who always switches language to adapt to others; she's always the one in the new situation, the "totally different environment." There are no examples where anyone has to adapt to her language. White students aren't bussed to black schools; white students don't have to write or learn Black English; "high class" people don't need to be "appropriate" in a "low class environment" because they don't often find themselves in such an environment and if they did they would expect others to adapt to their language. The English classroom is the epitome of a "totally different environment" where the language Ms. N is required to use parallels the language of a higher-class environment: "When we got around someone who was from a higher class environment, we would start speaking as if we were English majors." That Ms. N's background is a liability in the English classroom is a consequence of social relations between races, a political consequence, and also one felt immediately and personally by Ms. N.

Once we take into account the social and racial context of Ms. N's alteration of speech styles, I find it difficult to accept the easy-going attitude that Ms. N presents in this essay. She uses the word "appropriate" in the sentence, "Sometimes I feel that it is appropriate to change the way you use your language, especially when you are in a totally different environment." Her use of the word "appropriate" might just be an example of the very style change of which she speaks. In an effort to remove the bias that many students have, the attitude that academic English is inherently superior, I had lectured briefly in class on how various styles of speaking and writing are appropriate to various situations. I believe I unwittingly influenced Ms. N's writing up of her attitude towards language alteration. I don't believe that "appropriate" adequately describes the emotions that underlie Ms. N's language changes. Instead, it was a word that she felt would be "appropriate" for the educational context. When Ms. N gives examples of changing her language, such as with the English teacher who was "a real critic," she doesn't convey a sense of appropriateness at all. Instead, Ms. N seems to convey *resentment* at being coerced into an academic speech style. I get a similar sense from the phrase "we were taught a big lesson" when Ms. N recounts the experience of being bussed out, and in her use of the phrase "turned out." This resentment stems from Ms. N's perception of the roles of power among her white suburban schoolmates and her white teachers. She clearly understands that Standard English is the "prestige" form and while pragmatically deciding to alter her language to speak as "they" want to hear, she also reveals the anger and resentment that accompanies social coercion.

When we understand situational code switching as motivated by social pressure and Ms. N's compliance with this pressure as a part of her educational and social ambitions, we can then distinguish between the type of coercive situational code switching mentioned above and a very different type that Ms. N describes in her home life. Ms. N grew up in what she calls "the ghetto" in Chicago. Her father was an educator and a preacher; her mother was college-educated and employed. Ms. N says she was raised in a "Christian atmosphere." She mentions that her parents demanded a home language that differed from the language of her "regular gang"; they asked for a kind of code switching from street language to home language. Her description of this alteration of speech style highlights by contrast the resentful and angry emotions that accompany the similar change in school:

Going back to my second analytical essay I had discuss how I felt it was appropriate to change the way you use your language when you are around different people. I changed my features of language around my parents to show respect for what they stood for. I understood what my parents was teaching us but at the time I was not ready to settle down. So instead of upsetting my parents with my street language, I left that talk outside of their house and so did the rest of the family. We were not little angels but we did what we were told. . . . This was all done out of respect, the majority of my

family is very religious and you must speak the language they are custom to.
It is not that we put up an act in front of them pretending that we were so
good. They knew what we were doing and I would not ever lie to them telling
them I was not.

There is a much different tone in this description of language alteration
than in her description of "the real critic." Ms. N makes clear the reason
for her willingness to change: "respect." Additionally, she makes these
language changes in her home situation with honesty and openness, much
different attitudes from those that accompany the changes she makes for
English classes. In her home situation she claims, "It is not as if we put
up an act," but in the English classroom she writes that she was "putting
up a big front" when she changed style.

Did Ms. N "put up a big front" in my course? My answer to this difficult
question is an understandable (I hope) "yes and no." She did not write in
"street language"; her analytical papers, in my judgment, were thoroughly
"appropriate" for college writing. At least partially, she switched codes to
Standard English in my course. The related question, then, involves whether
she conceived of me on the basis of her experience with other English
teachers. Did I represent a part of that "totally different environment," or
did she conceive of me as something on the order of her parents, requiring
a language change, but a change based on values she could respect? I would
love to answer this question easily, saying that I broke the pattern of English
teachers and that Ms. N's success in her articulate rendering of the relationship between social groups and language was due to a productive
relationship based on mutual respect. Without a doubt, I did not fit her
expectations of English teachers. She mentioned several times her relief at
my not always correcting her writing. And I do think that we established
enough of a trusting relationship for her to be more honest in her writing
than her example of the forced "putting up a front" for the real critic. At
the same time this trust seemed occasional, intermittent. Although she
usually composed exceptional analytical papers, she wrote many of the public
essays in a perfunctory manner. Surely this indicates that the 23 white
students loomed large in her conception of audience, and short, nondescript
essays seemed safe. But I also believe that the conflict between Ms. N's
conception of English, connected as it is with a "high-class environment"
and coercive language practices, and my classroom practices, which possibly
indicated different language strategies, led her occasionally to trust me and
occasionally be skeptical of me. For instance, she claimed her papers were
formally simple: "I have been taught all my life in writing any kind of paper
always have an introduction, body and conclusion. I tried to stay with this
pattern and sometimes I do if I'm trying to impress somebody." These two
sentences contain some of the contradictions that lead me to my sense of

an intermittent trust. On one hand, she says her papers have introductions, bodies, and conclusions and she says she does that when she's trying to impress someone. Conclusion: She wrote in a conventional form to impress me. I didn't ask for a conventional form, nor do I believe that students' usual conception of such a form makes for effective writing, but Ms. N continued to act on her suspicions that, sooner or later, the real critic would come out. She embeds the voice of the teacher she was trying to impress in her own syntax, deleting either the "to" or the quotation marks in the phrase: "always have an introduction, body and conclusion." On the other hand, by honestly stating that her motivation for using the conventional form was strictly compliant (she didn't pretend that this form served a useful purpose), she stepped outside of the role of what Mr. C would call The Perfect Student.

Ms. N's use of Standard English is another example of these contradictory feelings of trust. Ms. N claimed all along that she *was able* to write in Standard English. Most of her essays, however, contained some features of Black English Vernacular, especially the deleted "s" on third person verb forms, the absence of possessive markers, and the deletion of the -ed on past tense verbs. These features are among the easiest to change; they follow fairly regular rules and I have no doubt that Ms. N could have easily written entirely in Standard English if she chose to. I did tell her that although these features didn't matter at all to me, and had nothing to do with her grade, other teachers might grade her down for their use and she should be aware of this. Her first analytical paper was entirely free from these forms and was, aside from typographic errors, written in Standard academic English (with an "introduction, body and conclusion"). After that, even through the final paper, Ms. N wrote using these three features of Black English Vernacular. She did not regularly employ any other features of Black English Vernacular; she did not delete the copula or employ the invariant be, for instance, although she did in her speech. She did not, therefore, write down her speech, or simply translate oral language into written. Why, then, didn't she write in full Standard English? I see her use of features of Black English Vernacular as similar to her transient flashes of true candor—as tests. She certainly proved that she could write in complete Standard English; she said as much (twice) and she did it, too (I am leaving aside the issue that I never asked her to write in Standard English). I think she was testing, in a relatively safe way, whether or not I was as good as my word. She was seeing, in other words, if I was going to turn into "the real critic" or not.

While Ms. N was occasionally and brilliantly honest and she was willing to take small risks to check whether or not I was trustworthy, the pattern of forced compliance with power, the sense that Ms. N had to abandon her home language for the language of school under conditions of criticism, correction, and ostracism was a major and negative influcnce on Ms. N's writing in my course. Through the process of education she has had to see her background as a liability, ignore it, or try to minimize its influence. These negative influences included a sense of limited choices of style, form, and expression, a limitation on the resources she felt she could use to gain an enriched understanding of language use, and, perhaps most damaging in the long run, a sense of despair about using written language productively in her life. Unlike Mr. H, in Chapter Three, who was able to harness compliance with the teacher and masculine motives together with a written style that satisfied his own sense of effective language, Ms. N knows that her own sense of language won't do in school; her language gets corrected and criticized. She doesn't see the possibility of combining her own motives and desires in language with the customs of the classroom as she constructed them. For really, nothing I did permanently dispelled Ms. N's image of the English teacher as constructed by her past experiences. Ms. N's choices remained the same in my classroom as they did in the "real critic's." Ms. N retained the perception that speaking authentically and in her own language would be met either with ridicule from the 23 white students or with a bad grade from me—or both. The only other possibility in the classroom, as she perceived it, was a forced compliance with the teacher. Ms. N wrote about these disturbing feelings with a degree of candor unusual for a student:

> While growing up I use to love to write. I wrote down all my feelings and thought. This was the best way I could express myself. I use to take my time and make sure that all my commas were in the right place and all my sentences were complete ones and not run ons. I always had to go back and double check and sometimes triple check that all my grammar were correct. I never could figure out why I made so many grammar errors and I knew all the rules for them and what to use and when to use them. Since I've been in college my whole outlook on writing has changed. Its gotten to the point where instead of me actually sitting down, thinking the situation or problem out that I have to write about, I just write what I feel the teacher might want to hear. Yes, I even done this in my class with you. . . . Writing has become like an enemy to me lately. . . .

This is a depressing account of English teaching. As you might imagine, it is particularly depressing to me: "Yes, I even done this in my class with you." Yet I find it perfectly clear why writing has become an enemy to her. Although I asked her to draw on her especially rich background to provide her with an understanding of how she uses language, this request did not occur in isolation. She heard this request as part of the history of experiences with English teachers. And if she hadn't cited English teachers, she could have cited others; there is a country full of people who believe that black speech is evidence of inabilities: the inability to analyze, the inability to be logical, the inability to concentrate, the inability to be serious, the inability to work hard, the inability to be precise. And while I certainly learned a great deal from Ms. N—I learned to anticipate mistrust—I didn't make writing an enemy to her.

The lesson here is that English teachers are both powerful and not-so-powerful. One can see in Ms. N's history the sense of influence that teachers have had on her, and it is unfortunately negative. One can also see that I didn't achieve the influence I wished, despite not conforming to her expectations of what a teacher was going to do. The issues are numbers and force, and in Ms. N's experience, I was a minority of one. Commenting on the potential of English teachers for social action, Geneva Smitherman (1977) asserts with characteristic energy and certainty:

> The teacher can definitely be an agent of social change. But it is not enough to work in the classroom alone. That is a necessary but not sufficient task. Inasmuch as teachers form part of the institutional fabric of the school, they help to shape the character and style of that institution. (p. 234)

My reason for telling Ms. N's story is to contribute to shaping the character and style of the institution, to increase the numbers and force of those who will reject deficit theory or "residual" deficit theories. Pedagogy based on these theories isolates students from the strengths of their backgrounds and needlessly limits the possibilities for rewarding explorations into language use. These pedagogies, according to Smitherman, are not designed to

> instill pride in Black language and culture, nor to teach black students critical thinking and analysis, nor, above all, to give them tools to righteously examine the socioeconomic workings of America. (p. 203)

In the place of deficit theories, we need a language pedagogy that conceives of students as contributors, as people with valuable social and linguistic backgrounds that can help their understanding of reading and writing, as people who, if the learning context permits, have the ability to think critically and analytically about language use.

6
Teachers Don't Teach Alone

These case studies together suggest that by studying the most obvious and widespread demarcations of inequality (gender, class, and race), a writing class can explore the ways in which education and culture silences or transforms resistance and inhibits students from disclosing their full humanity. Ms. M, for instance, in refusing to write about anything controversial, used language in the classroom that misrepresented her intelligence and analytical abilities. She became aware, during the course, of the ways that gender relations contributed to this misrepresentation. Mr. C's refrain that all social groups were equal concealed his concern that he might not be treated equally and inhibited his own ability to deeply address issues of class. What changed for each of these students was a new recognition of the role that language plays in signalling and creating boundaries of privilege and the effects this role has on learning. This recognition was brought about by a focused *interpretative* attention to their own and each other's language.

INTERPRETATION IN WRITING COURSES

Recent literary theory has called attention to the centrality of interpretation in literature studies. Even stylistic descriptions of literary texts and the evaluation of the canon rest on interpretative acts, acts shaped by membership in educational institutions (and therefore shaped by training in educational institutions) and membership in social groups (as demonstrated by feminist, Marxist, and other politically minded critics). Although scholarship in composition, as in all scholarship in language, has been interpretative, much of it has only been reluctantly interpretative, and the interpretation of student writing has yet to be institutionalized as pedagogy in most composition courses. Perhaps because composition lacks the prestige that literary studies hold, much research has shied away from interpretation towards more quantifiable and therefore more "scientific" projects. Mike Rose, in two recent articles, "The Language of Exclusion" (1985) and "Narrowing the Mind and the Page" (1988), has shown that this focus has resulted in reducing our estimation of the complexity—the

109

humanity—of our students. Even when interpretation becomes central, as in Mina Shaughnessy's (1977) and some of David Barthomolomae's (1985) work, the teacher is the only researcher in town.[1]

But interpretation of what? And interpretation to what ends? My study suggests both the pedagogical and political advantages of interpreting how the social fault lines of our society shape acts of literacy, and how interpreting acts of literacy can be critical and liberating, enlarging the worlds of our students. The interpretative frame of this study concentrates on the sources of conflict in our culture, sources of conflict that are equally present in classrooms and schools. In schools and classrooms, however, and in particular those classrooms devoted to teaching literacy, these conflicts remain for the most part unexamined. They are buried by institutional organization or obscured by philosophical orientations of individualism and behaviorism.

The most obvious and important conceptual change in training teachers of writing is to replace evaluation as the central concern of literacy instruction and move interpretation to the core. *Both* teachers and students must primarily be preoccupied with understanding the meaning and uses of literacy. Shaping the interpretation of writing are the students' experience, both educational and social, and the present classroom context itself—the double context of the case studies. Teachers in training need to be less preoccupied with classroom management and fair evaluation and more concerned with a day-to-day understanding of students. Interpretation is, of course, never itself unshaped, and a frame of some sort always determines meaning. The frame, I argue, should be shaped by our most urgent problem in education and society, which is now the continuing inability for education to work democratically.

Since students understand who they can be in the classroom by what they have experienced in classrooms, teachers need to know how the particular disciplinary history of writing and reading have formed the way we think of our tasks, and how we might think of them. Although

---

[1] Mina Shaughnessy's *Errors and Expectations* (1977) provides all writing teachers with a model of inductive, interpretative work on student writing. David Bartholomae and Patricia Bizzell have broadened Shaughnessy's work by focusing less on individual writer's strategies of error and more on showing how student texts mark a discourse community. See David Bartholomae, "Inventing the University" (1986); Patricia Bizzell "What Happens When Basic Writers Come to College" (1986b).

Two notable works explore students' interpretations of their own writing: David Bleich's most recent work, *The Double Perspective* (1988) and David Bartholomae and Anthony Petrosky's *Facts, Counterfacts, and Artifacts* (1986). Both works describe theoretical and pedagogical projects that take interpretation as the central activity of the classroom, both take seriously the interpretation of student writing, and—most importantly—both involve the student in the active interpretation of his or her own work.

disciplinary history is a relatively new concern, there are already materials available: James Berlin's two histories of writing instruction, *Writing Instruction in Nineteenth-Century American Colleges* (1984) and *Rhetoric and Reality: Writing Instruction in American Colleges, 1900–1985* (1987), and Gerald Graff's history of English departments, *Professing Literature* (1987), are good starts.[2] Knowledge of institutional history and the social forces that help define it provide teachers with a general interpretative frame from which they can seek to understand the relationship between themselves, their students, and the day-to-day classroom practices. Although beginning teachers, with beginning anxiety, wish for what Ann Berthoff (1981) calls "recipes," these recipes ultimately contribute to "deskilling" and reduce teachers' political power and their ability to determine their own classroom. Knowledge about the historical construction of teachers and classroom activities gives teachers both the knowledge and the authority to determine their own classrooms.

TWO TEXTS

Two texts by feminists will help me explore the kinds of changes that my study suggest are necessary, Virginia Woolf's *Three Guineas* (1938) and Dale Spender's "Education: The Patriarchal Paradigm and the Response to Feminism" (1981). I cite Virginia Woolf's *Three Guineas,* her extended essay considering the connections among pacificism, feminism, and education, not for any specific programmatic change she suggests, but for the kind of relational and critical thinking that teachers, from the beginning of their careers to the end, need to be engaged in. I'll begin with a remarkable passage where Woolf contemplates donating a guinea to help rebuild a women's college. She imagines the college's curriculum, one that takes advantage of two of the qualities of such a college: youth and poverty.

> It should teach the arts of human intercourse; the art of understanding other people's lives and minds, and the little arts of talk, of dress, of cookery that are allied with them. The aim of the new college, the cheap college, should not segregate and specialize, but to combine. It should . . . discover what new combinations make good wholes in human life. (p. 34)

Woolf's speculation on a curriculum free from "the arts of dominating other people" is interesting enough. Among other things, she seeks understanding

---

[2] See also Mike Rose, "The Language of Exclusion: Writing Instruction at the University" (1985) for an example of how disciplinary history affects pedagogy.

of daily language use, an interpretative focus on everyday life. These speculations are interrupted by the imagined author of the request, the honorary treasurer of the building fund for the women's college. Woolf imagines her saying " 'Dream your dreams . . . fire off your rhetoric, but we have to face realities' " (p. 35). The reality that the honorary treasurer faces includes the fact that her graduates need to get jobs, and to get jobs they need a regular degree. Thus, by economic necessity, the women's college must be rebuilt on the model of the men's, it needs to

> make Research produce practical results which will induce bequests and donations from rich men; it must encourage competition; it must accept degrees and coloured hoods; it must accumulate great wealth; it must exclude other people from a share of its wealth. . . . (p. 35)

So Woolf concludes, "No guinea of earned money should go to rebuilding the college on the old plan . . ." (p. 36). Then in prose as powerful as anywhere in the book, Woolf decides to earmark the guinea:

> "Rags. Petrol. Matches." And this note should be attached to it. "Take this guinea and with it burn the college to the ground. Set fire to the old hypocrisies. Let the light of the burning building scare the nightingales and incarnadine the willows. And let the daughters of educated men dance round the fire and heap armful upon armful of dead leaves upon the flames. And let their mothers lean from the upper windows and cry, 'Let it blaze! Let it blaze! For we have done with this "education"!' " (p. 36)

After asserting that the passage is not "empty rhetoric," Woolf also acknowledges that if the daughters of educated men could not obtain appointments they would "again be dependent upon their fathers and brothers" and her political aims of freedom and the eradication of war through changed education would not be accomplished.

Woolf ultimately decides to give the guinea to the building fund without conditions. But she also asserts that her own participation in education has conditions. She argues for a critical understanding of curriculum: "If we are asked to teach, we can examine very carefully into the aim of such teaching, and refuse to teach any art or science that encourages war" (pp. 36–37). Additionally, Woolf refuses to participate in the various competitions that men's education involves, pouring "mild scorn" upon degrees and the value of examinations, maintaining that "a book may still be worth reading in spite of the fact that its author took a first class with honours in the English tripos" (p. 37).

The conflict between the "reality" of jobs and degrees is replayed in the present-day tensions between writing courses as "service" courses and writing courses that conceive of themselves as part of the discipline of writing. Woolf dives into such conflicts and provides us with a model of the complexity and courage with which teachers and students must think about education. We must be willing, at times, to at least figuratively think "Rags. Petrol. Matches," if only to rethink and rearticulate our present educational goals and practices. Woolf was writing as an outsider, admitting her influence could be, at best, "indirect." Although teachers and students sometimes feel like outsiders in their own educations, our influence need not be indirect.

Dale Spender's exploration of feminist education in "Education: The Patriarchal Paradigm and the Response to Feminism," written 40 years after *Three Guineas,* continues Woolf's themes. Spender writes from a social constructionist point of view, but unlike Bruffee (1986) (see Chapter 1), Spender sees "social" complexly, reflecting social habits that stratify men and women. And since "social" is stratified, it follows that the knowledge that society privileges by teaching it in school has been produced by the privileged social group. Thus, knowledge taught in school reflects a patriarchal bias. As feminism's latest surge picked up steam in the 1970s, women came to realize that school knowledge was at best partial, at worst false. And since this predated much of the important rediscovery of feminist history, indeed the history of women's contributions in all disciplines, women were left to their own resources: "If the knowledge produced by men was inadequate or false then there was no alternative but to set up a 'circle of women' to produce and validate knowledge about women" (p. 167).

These historical circumstances, the lack of received, canonical knowledge about women and the politically urgent need for it, led to a new form of education: "By placing this emphasis on personal experience and validation, they formed the basis of an educational model which constituted a radical departure from traditional education and which still distinguishes feminism from patriarchal education" (p. 167).

The serious and critical focus on personal experience has (at least) two consequences: It made knowledge collective not competitive, and it placed interpretation, not evaluation or skills that could be measured, at the center. Learning had to be a collective enterprise for a number of reasons, primarily for political and personal strength. But practically speaking, since at that time feminists had little printed history to draw upon, knowledge had to come from widespread sharing of personal experience:

> Connections were made, critiques developed, analyses undertaken, explanations offered and verified, as women checked with women about the collective nature of their experience. New knowledge was produced in a different way; it was 'collective' knowledge, 'made' rather than 'received' by all those who participated. (p. 167)

Secondly, and equally important, feminist education changed the mental acts of education, from the memorization and elaboration of patriarchal education to synthesis, critique, analysis, verification, and explanation. These mental acts supplant the mania for evaluation, making ridiculous traditional education's preoccupations with judgment:

> many of the traditional theories of teaching and learning, motivation and memorisation, appear most inappropriate. For women who have participated in feminist education it is not necessary to make a conscious effort to commit to memory the fact of oppression; it is not as if they are likely to forget— or even to be 'tested' on what they know! While learning is so closely linked with living, as it is within feminism, the premise that it is necessary to introduce external factors to induce human beings to learn, and to help them retain what they could learn, seems inapplicable. (p. 169)

All learning, if we retain any dignity in the term, must be linked with living. Because we conduct our daily lives in language, learning about language has a particular obligation to be linked with living.

JUDGMENT

Most feminist education during the era Spender discusses occurred outside of the classroom. Although there's been an enormous growth of feminist classes in the university, especially through women's studies programs, feminist learning styles have not really influenced most classrooms. One of the facts that stands out in the case studies is the enormous effect that "judgment" by both peers and teacher has on student writing. Ms. M, in fact, withdrew the meaningful contributions she could have made to the classroom collective for fear of "ridicule;" Mr. H was so concerned about the teacher's judgment, a concern motivated by competition, that he never really concentrated on either understanding or being understood. Contributing to the socially constructed knowledge of a community was irrelevant to the education he believed he was engaged in. He assumed from the beginning that when he "stated his opinions as facts" they would be understood as facts. Mr. C's theme of judgment prevented him, for most of the semester, from exploring the meaningful differences and similarities between social groups. Finally, Ms. N's experience with the "real critics" in her education shaped her image of me, and thus her writing, so that she hesitated to trust a course that seemed, in part, to appeal to her interests in language.

The concern with judgment interferes not only with the work that problem-posing teachers wish to accomplish, it interferes with the desires of students to enact their humanity in the classroom. Because the preoccupation flows from two related sources—educational practices that stress individuality and universality and social practices that stratify people on the basis of gender, class, and race—"judgment" is a particularly recalcitrant problem.

Classroom practices from kindergarten on work to stratify children, usually on the basis of an objective test's judgment of ability. "Ability-based" reading groups begin in the first years and continue throughout a child's education. Children quickly learn that reading and writing is something that one is good or better at and not a collective occasion for making meaning. Judgment, by teachers and peers, supercedes the use of writing and reading for the discovery of knowledge or the communication of meaning. Much teacher-training, at present, concentrates on the supposedly fair and accurate discrimination of students on a single standard of ability. Students, conversely, concentrate on figuring out how to beat the system of evaluation, and the texts they create are based on that. Each student in this study created texts for a grade, and the degree of success that we achieved rested only on the complementarity of my political and pedagogical goals, students' intentions, and their interpretation of the teacher's wishes.

INTERPRETING THE CLASSROOM

If interpretation were central to the language classroom, then "understanding," not judgment would be the dominant focus. I have been arguing all along that one cannot separate educational practices from social ones, and judgments in classroom contexts connect with social judgments, usually based on gender, class, or racial privilege. Ms. M's concern lay mostly with the judgments of her male peers, while Mr. H did not ever consider the judgment of his female subgroup, only the teacher. Both case studies suggest that gender roles coincide with educational ones. Mr. C and Ms. N believed their class and racial backgrounds might cause me to judge them negatively, lowering or changing my expectations. Both sought, in different ways, to use writing as a means of obscuring their backgrounds and thus overcoming those judgments.

All of the work that students do to seek equality in the classroom, while cognitively complex, is work that could have been done to contribute to the knowledge of the teachers and other students. Much classroom work—of interpretation, negotiation, creation—is a hidden response to what radical educators have called the hidden curriculum.[3] One of Woolf's suggestions, "to very carefully examine the aims of teaching," ought to be a part of every classroom and every teacher training program. Because we collectively produce knowledge, no single curriculum nor any set of assignments could remove any single classroom from the educational context as it is now constructed. While this fact may tempt one with the "Rags. Petrol. Matches." solution, it also overlooks the power of school to encourage resistance. The resistance that Giroux and others claim is ever-present is sometimes difficult to see in my classroom and in the classrooms of my friends and colleagues. When students achieve some real understanding of the uses of literacy in their lives, this usually occurs as a result of an alliance with me, not resistance to me; students perceive that I don't like what's going on in education either. Up until that point of trust, I observe mostly compliance or very passive opposition; it's hard to tell the difference. But Giroux is absolutely right in stressing the potential for the classroom and the school to be transformative. I don't believe that can happen without a double curriculum that corresponds to the two sources of judgment that so affect my students. This curriculum must address both the inequalities that exist outside the classroom and the effect those inequalities have on literacy, *and* a concurrent focus on classroom activities and procedures. Students and teachers must both be continually interpreting and critiquing the classroom as it evolves. Students and teachers already do this all the time, just as we interpret and critique everyday conversations. But especially in the classroom, these activities are kept guardedly secret. Students do not "let on how much they really know," because they may need to show "progress" for evaluation and they will not disclose how they have figured out what the teacher wants because teachers have a habit of changing what they want once a student figures it out. Teachers, of course, cannot disclose their interpretation of the classroom because that act immediately diminishes their omnipotence.

This habit of mutual miscommunication and misinformation takes advantage of none of the real opportunities for learning that the classroom could present. This is why classroom conversations, reading and writing assignments, and grading procedures (if one must grade) ought to be examined by students and teachers with the same seriousness as the content of the course. A major part of this exploration of classroom practices needs to be the study of the hierarchical nature of student-teacher relationships and how those hierarchies are enforced through grading or through other means. And students themselves, along with the teacher, should explore how hierarchies inside the classroom relate to

---

[3] For a discussion of the concept of the hidden curriculum, see Henry A. Giroux, *Ideology, Culture and the Process of Schooling* (1981), especially pp. 72–79.

hierarchies outside the classroom. For if language use is as radically contextual as recent theory would have it, classroom language itself is the most reliable instance of language to analyze.

Since classroom language itself is the most reliable instance of language to analyze, and since, according to Ohmann, Spender, and others, the histories of classroom practices exclude social and political questions, an interactive classroom that seeks to explore political questions in language use at home and in school is bound to run into problems. What surprised me most in conducting this study was the difficulty of truly teaching this course at all, although in retrospect I can easily enough see the problem. I expected to find that gender, class, and race affected my students' language use in the classroom, and I expected that students would find my course strange, for I knew it differed from the usual freshman composition course. I also knew that, as a required course, many students would simply pass their time in the course, complying with my requests whether or not they were strange. These students would simply be jumping through hoops, but at least (I rationalized), the process of jumping through these particular hoops might be a valuable one. But some students did not even comply with my wishes to examine their language politically. They instead complied with what they thought were my real wishes, my real agenda, which looked like the one they expected: the perfection of a narrow conception of academic writing. I don't think this is the resistance that Giroux talks about, although I tried to pursue it hoping that the issue of compliance with an imaginary (or historical) teacher could be articulated. These students weren't dense, nor was I particularly inept in dealing with them. Nor do they discount the successes I had in the class.

CONFLICT AT THE CENTER

Resistance to the political frame may simply be the force of habit, a sincere belief in what compositions courses do (they are skills classes where one learns to write for school) and a determination to accomplish that goal. In other cases, however, the resistance is more complex, and more like what Giroux, Willis, and others see as transformative. This kind of resistance, best shown in Chapter Five's case study of Ms. N, grows from a skepticism of education in general, and not from an overly certain faith. This kind of skepticism grows from an antagonistic education, an education that has not only not been relevant to the experiences of its students, but has actually seen students' experiences as liabilities.

Ms. N's experiences in getting "turned out" by the white students after she was bussed to the suburbs and her experiences with the "real critic" represent an individual's experience of what Ogbu calls "oppositional culture" and show how oppositional cultures affect an effort to combine home and school. When home and school have been traditionally in conflict, any request to combine them is likely to be met with skepticism. Literacy is so closely tied with the idea of school in our culture that reading and writing activities themselves symbolize school for many students. The opposition of school and culture is certainly a more complex problem than a one semester course can address. However, Ms. N—and to a certain extent Ms. M and Mr. C—suggest contours of change. To bring home and school cultures together, teachers and students must work in both arenas. Obviously, the social, economic, and intellectual gains that are supposed to be associated with education must be delivered. The ongoing fight against deep forces of racism, classism, and sexism ought to have education at its center. I hope that this study helps bring into focus some of the consequences of these forces on the educational performances of students and thus encourages political action and involvement by teachers and students. At the same time, change has to occur within the classroom. And one change that can be made is to develop approaches to teaching literacy that are forcibly *not* in opposition to the experiences of minority, women, and working-class students.

This book has taken for granted the integration of reading with writing. There has been enough written to theoretically support this decision, which has common sense to most teachers.[4] The question of what to read and for what purposes remains. Literary theorists have been arguing for expanding and reshaping the canon, those texts which our profession has deemed worthy of study. Feminist critics and other politically focused critics have argued forcefully that minority writers and women writers have been excluded from the canon due to racism and sexism. In addition the reasons of equal representation, when teachers of reading and writing include texts by blacks, women, and working-class writers, we *show* student from oppositional cultures a connection between their experience and acts of literacy. This act must be obvious and serious, a palpable demonstration of the connections between literacy and oppositional culture, a refutation of the students' expectation that school threatens cultural identity. Of course, more than simply adding texts by blacks, women, and working-class authors is required. Both the texts and students' experiences must be legitimated by the teachers' everyday acts and officially by the structure of the class.

Texts and classroom practices help fight the perception (and reality in many cases) that schools oppose minority cultures. But, as Virginia Woolf keenly felt, there are "realities" to face. "Reality" is usually invoked by

---

[4] See Bruce Peterson (Ed.), *Convergences* (1986) and Thomas Newkirk, *Only Connect* (1986).

those who wish for writing classes to fall more closely in line with the needs of competency tests or employment opportunities in business. We must not forget the other reality: Minority, women, and working-class students are at present ill-served by education. Still, writing classrooms exist as one class among others, and we must not mistake changing a classroom for changing education. The knowledge gained from the type of course I've described in this book most certainly differs from the knowledge gained in a more conventional course. There's no doubt about it: The knowledge about how education, social groups, and literacy styles intersect is not only different from other courses, it is sometimes in *conflict* with them. This is as much a conflict on any given individual campus as it is a conflict in our profession itself. Fundamentally, it places those who believe that writing courses are essentially service courses, whose content should be determined by the needs of the university and whose primarily aim is the transmissions of *skills,* in conflict with those who believe that writing is a discipline itself, and writing courses are *about* writing. The service course subsumes political conflicts by foregrounding pragmatic, adaptive strategies. The writing course embraces those exact conflicts.

Frequently, the most productive work of a discipline occurs during times when conflicts are openly discussed and written about. Yet, as Gerald Graff in *Professing Literature* (1987) argues, students don't get the benefit of these instructive conflicts. We tend, in Graff's words, to assume "that students should be exposed only to the *results* of the controversies of their teachers and educators and should be protected from the controversies themselves" (p. 261). To make an interpretative classroom work, we ought to bring both the conflicts of our society and the conflicts of our profession inside the classroom. Students, in such a case, would be doing real work; they could see that they really do have a say in their education, and we would not be ignoring the so-called "reality" of institutional and economic demands for these issues themselves would be a part of our instruction.

TEACHERS DON'T TEACH ALONE

We need not get depressed about the enormity of the changes necessary to make education transformative. Certainly there is much to do inside and outside schools. More than banking on a latent or unarticulated resistance among students and teachers, we need to recognize the valuable, progressive efforts of our colleagues.

Teachers never teach alone. Although there is characteristically only one teacher per classroom, that teacher is always a composite. The ghost of the "real critic" plagues every teacher of English and no classroom practices or ghostbusting assignments can obliterate it. The goal, at times an impossibility, is not for teachers to pretend to teach outside of history, but with increased awareness of this historical role, begin to find ways to stretch its boundaries.

The necessity for teachers to work collectively in this process is underscored a number of times in my study. Shirley Brice Heath returned to the Piedmont to find that teachers had abandoned the innovative roles that Heath had taught them; the brevity of the experiment was enforced by these teachers' isolation. Certainly, they taught and learned together, but a small circumscribed community is nearly as vulnerable as an individual teacher. The voice of a history of educational practices across the country is louder and more enduring than a group of very interesting teachers in the Piedmont. We can easily hear this voice in my study, too, in Ms. N's statement, "I just write what I feel the teacher might want to hear," in Mr. C's self-presentation as "The Perfect Student," in the student who understood my comments as "a good way to spot flaws;" the voice reverberates in some form in every students' language and no doubt in my habits of language, too. No individual teacher's classroom practices will solve these problems.

The reasons to change these educational practices are clear. By conceiving of students only as Individuals and Students, and by concentrating on evaluation based on this conception, conventional practices inhibit the success of women, working-class, and minority students. Academic success often exacts a price from those who do manage to succeed, the necessity to suppress one's background. These practices result in excluding many students from economic and social privileges and work to deny them the strength that comes from understanding oneself as belonging to a group. The advantages of exploring social backgrounds in language study lies in achieving the political goals I stated in Chapter One: a tolerant understanding of diverse social groups and enlarging the worlds of those who have been denied social privileges.

Although the voice of the historical teacher is a strong one, there are other voices to listen to. This study is no more the product of individual teacher than are the student essays products of individual students. It grew from experiences with other teachers at Indiana University and the California State University, from teachers in my educational history, and from teachers like Heath, Freire, Spender, Kozol, Ohmann, Bleich, Smitherman, and others who wrote down their thoughts. This study also grew from interactions with people outside academic life, from my wife and children, my parents, siblings, and friends, all of whom taught me in everyday interactions. Learning from these "teachers" in everyday life is perhaps the best model for an interactive classroom, for this kind of learning takes place in an interaction between people who matter to each other. When teachers and students matter to each other, learning can begin to involve the great issues of oppression, prejudice, inequality. These issues, as my study indicates, affect everyday interaction inside and outside of the classroom, despite a history of classroom practices, textbooks, and theories of reading and writing that have excluded conscious attention to them. This exclusion prevents reading and writing instruction from being linked to the world and to students' lives. I intend in this book to contribute to the strength of the voices of teachers and students that taught me, voices that speak for involving teaching, learning, and language use in the political and social world.

Appendix

I intend the following list of assignments to give the reader an idea of the progression of this course and how the syllabus reflects my political convictions. There is always a danger in including such information: that it will be perceived as the most important aspect because it is the most easily apprehended. These assignments should not be seen as suggestions for paper topics. More important than the actual assignments are the principles of interaction between student and teacher that do not rely on any specific paper topic. These assignments do, however, help to communicate an attitude and provide a context for my discussion of students' work.

STUDYING SOCIAL GROUPS AND LITERACY

Introduction

Essay 1
Write an essay telling the class who you are. Be as thorough as time allows.

Gender and Language

Essay 2
Tell about an instance where someone said (or wrote) something that seemed to you to be characteristic of the opposite sex. Explain your relationship to the other person and why you thought it was typical of the opposite sex.

Essay 3
Read carefully Hawthorne's "The Birthmark." In a 3-page (minimum) essay tell which character(s) you most closely identified with and which character(s) you identified with least. Then think about the feelings that accompanied your identifications or lack of identifications. Name the feelings, then write of a time in your own history where you might have had similar feelings. With two different identifications, you may want to tell about two different experiences.

Essay 4

Read carefully Glaspell's "A Jury of Her Peers." In a 3-page (minimum) essay tell which character(s) you most closely identified with and which character(s) you identified with least. Then think about the feelings that accompanied your identifications or lack of identifications. Name the feelings, then write of a similar time in your own history where you might have had similar feelings. With two different identifications, you may want to tell about two different experiences.

Analytical Paper 1

Compare and contrast your language system with the language system of *one* of your subgroup members. Describe as many important language features as you can. Make some guesses about the intentions each of these features expresses, paying special attention to recurring language features or recurring intentions. Explain these features and intentions in terms of "masculinity" and "femininity." Be sure to consider the following issues: (1) the writer's attitude or "stance" towards his or her audience (2) the writer's identifications in "The Birth-mark" and "A Jury of Her Peers" (3) the writer's relationships in her or his own history.

Use essays 1–4 plus any observations made during class discussions and subgroups meetings. Feel free to contact your subgroup members for help, if you wish. Make sure to document your statements with examples from the essays or from class discussions and subgroup meetings. *Note that this assignment requires you to make claims about both your language system and the language system of a subgroup member.*

Ethnicity and Language

Essay 5

What was your most important experience with prejudice? Tell about the incident, what was said or done, who was involved and why it was significant for you. (1-½ pages minimum)

Essay 6

Tell what you think is the most important passage or episode in *Their Eyes Were Watching God.* Name the passage and why you think it was important. Then tell what feelings you experienced while reading it or thinking about it. Name the feelings and then write about an experience in your own life where you think you had similar feelings.

Essay 7

Tell what you think is the most important passage or episode in "Benito Cereno." Name the passage and why you think it was important. Then tell what feelings you experienced while reading it or thinking about it. Name the feelings and then write about an experience in your own life where you think you had similar feelings. Minimum length: three pages.

Analytical Paper 2
Compare and contrast your language system with the language system of the subgroup member on whom you did not write last time. Concentrate on essays 5–7, but feel free to examine all of the essays. In this paper, look carefully at *recurring* language features and intentions, and try to sum up how ethnic backgrounds and attitudes affect your reading and writing and the reading and writing of the subgroup member. Remember you must examine both your language system and the language system of the subgroup member. As always, use plenty of well-chosen examples to support your claims.

Class and Language

Essay 8
Recall an experience where you realized that you were from a different social or economic class than someone else. Tell about the situation, the people involved, and how you made this realization.

Essay 9
Read *Life in the Iron Mills*. After you are done, think over your reading experience and try to cite the moment when you experienced the strongest feelings, whatever they may be. Name and describe the feelings and cite the exact passage in the text. Then give an example of a time in your own history where you experienced similar feelings. Note that I am not asking you to name a time in your life when you were in the same situation as the one you cited in the book, just a time when you had the same feelings.

Essay 10
Read Hemingway's "The Doctor and the Doctor's Wife." Think over your reading experience and decide at what point in the story you had the strongest feelings. Name the feeling and cite the exact passage in the text. Explain why you from you own life where you think you experienced similar feelings. 3–5 pages.

Analytical Paper 3
Summarize your understanding of how social and economic class influence your language system. Pay particular attention to the issues of authority and power as they relate to your language use. Look at *all* your essays, but concentrate on essays 8–10.

For the second part of the paper, see if your conclusions about your language use in the first part of your paper apply to how you use language in your subgroup, again, paying particular attention to issues of power and authority. Explain why you think your conclusions apply or why they do not. This assignment requires you to characterize the typical language habits of your subgroup members. Since you have written an analytical paper on each of the other members of the group, it makes sense to refer to these papers to explain their typical roles, but feel free to go beyond your conclusions in AP 1 and 2.

Final Paper (excerpt)

The aim of this paper is to describe and explain, as much as possible, your language use. The materials for this project are your essays, your analytical papers, your class participation, your subgroup interaction, and any other information you may wish to introduce.

The best final papers almost always focus on a theme or a set of related themes in the author's work. This theme provides the perspective through which all the categories of language features are discussed. Because we have emphasized the roles that gender, ethnicity, and social class play in language use, it is likely that your theme will, at least partly, be connected to these social categories.

References

Apple, Michael. (1983). Curricular form and the logic of technical control. In M. Apple & L. Weis (Eds.), *Ideology and practice in schooling.* Philadelphia: Temple University Press.

Aronowitz, Stanley, & Giroux, Henry A. (1985). *Education under seige.* South Hadley, MA: Bergin and Garvey.

Austin, J. L. (1962). *How to do things with words* (2nd ed.). Cambridge: Harvard University Press.

Bartholomae, David. (1985). Inventing the university. In M. Rose (Ed.), *When a writer can't write.* New York: Guilford Press.

Bartholomae, David, & Petrosky, Anthony. (1986). *Facts, artifacts, and counterfacts.* Upper Montclair, NJ: Boyton/Cook.

Beck, Evelyn Torton. (1983). Self-disclosure and commitment to social change. *Women's Studies International Forum, 6,* 159–163.

Bereiter, Carl, & Englemann, Siegfried. (1966). *Teaching disadvantaged children in the preschool.* Englewood Cliffs, NJ: Prentice-Hall.

Berlin, James. (1984). *Writing instruction in nineteenth-century American colleges.* Carbondale, IL: Southern Illinois Press.

Berlin, James. (1987). *Rhetoric and reality: Writing instruction in American colleges, 1900-1985.* Carbondale, IL: Southern Illinois Press.

Bernstein, Basil. (1977). *Class, codes, and control, I.* London: Routledge and Kegan Paul.

Berthoff, Ann E. (1981). *The making of meaning.* Montclair, NJ: Boyton/ Cook.

Bissex, Glynda, & Bullock, R. (1987). *Seeing for ourselves: Case study research by teachers of writing.* Portsmouth, NH: Heinemann.

Bizzell, Patricia. (1982). Cognition, convention, and certainty: What we need to know about writing. *Pre/Text, 3,* 213–44.

Bizzell, Patricia. (1986a). Foundationalism and anti-foundationalism in composition studies. *Pre/Text, 7,* 37–56.

Bizzell, Patricia. (1986b). What happens when basic writers come to college? *College Composition and Communication, 37,* 294–301.

Bleich, David. (1975). *Readings and feelings: An introduction to subjective criticism.* Urbana, IL: National Council of Teachers of English.

Bleich, David. (1978). *Subjective criticism.* Baltimore: Johns Hopkins University Press.

Bleich, David. (1986). Intersubjective reading. *New Literary History, 17,* 401–421.

Bleich, David. (1988). *The double perspective: Language, literacy, and social relations.* New York: Oxford University Press.

Bourdieu, Pierre, & Passeron, J. P. (1977). *Reproduction in education, society, and culture.* Beverly Hills, CA: Sage.

Bowles, S., & Gintis, H. (1976). *Schooling in capitalist America.* New York: Basic Books.

Brannon, Lil, & Knoblauch, C.H. (1982). On students' rights to their own texts: A model of teacher response. *College Composition and Communication, 33,* 157–66.

Brodkey, Linda. (1987). Writing critical ethnographic narratives. *Anthropology and Education Quarterly, 18,* 67–76.

Bruffee, Kenneth. (1984). Peer tutoring and the "Conversation of Mankind." In Gary Olson (Ed.), *Writing centers: Theory and administration.* Urbana, IL: National Council of Teachers of English.

Bruffee, Kenneth. (1986). Social construction, language and the authority of knowledge. *College English, 48,* 773–790.

Conference on College Composition and Communication. (1974). Students' right to their own language. *College Composition and Communication, 25.*

Cook-Gumperz, Jenny. (Ed.). (1986). *The social construction of literacy.* Cambridge: Cambridge University Press.

Cook-Gumperz, Jenny & Gumperz, John J. (1981). From oral to written culture: The transition to literacy. In Marcia Farr Whiteman (Ed.), *Writing, Vol. 1: Variation in writing.* Hillsdale, NJ: Lawrence Erlbaum.

Culler, Jonathon. (1975). *Structuralist poetics.* Ithaca: Cornell University Press.

Culler, Jonathon. (1981). *The pursuit of signs.* Ithaca: Cornell University Press.

Culler, Jonathan. (1982). *On deconstruction: Theory and criticism after structuralism.* Ithaca: Cornell University Press.

Daeumer, Elisabeth. (1985). Gender bias in the concept of audience. *Reader, 13,* 32–41.

Davis, Rebecca Harding. (1972). *Life in the iron mills.* New York: The Feminist Press. (Original work published 1861)

Derrida, Jacques. (1977). Signature event context. *Glyph, 1,* 172–97.

Deutsch, Martin & Associates. (1967). *The disadvantaged child.* New York: Basic Books.

Dittmar, Norbert. (1976). *Sociolinguistics.* (Peter Sand, Pieter Seuren, and Kevin Whitely, Trans.). London: Edward Arnold.

Elsasser, Nan, & John-Steiner, Vera P. (1977). An interactionalist approach to advancing literacy. *Harvard Educational Review, 47,* 355-699.

Farrell, Thomas. (1983). IQ and standard English. *College Composition and Communication, 34,* 470-84.

Farrell, Thomas, & Sledd, James. (1984). Comment and response. *College English, 46,* 822-829.

Fetterly, Judith. (1978). *The resisting reader.* Bloomington: Indiana University Press.

Flynn, Elizabeth. (1983a). Gender and reading. *College English, 45,* 236-253.

Flynn, Elizabeth. (1983b). Women as reader-response critics. *New Orleans Review, 10,* 20-25.

Fish, Stanley. (1980). *Is there a text in this class?* Cambridge: Harvard University Press.

Freire, Paulo. (1983). *Pedagogy of the oppressed.* (Myra Bergman Ramos, Trans.). New York: Continuum. (Original work published 1970)

Frye, Marilyn. (1983). *The politics of reality: Essays on feminist theory.* Trumansburg, NY: Crossing Press.

Garfinkel, Harold. (1967). *Studies in ethnomethodology.* Englewood Cliffs, NJ: Prentice Hall.

Geertz, Clifford. (1973). *The interpretation of cultures.* New York: Basic Books.

Gilligan, Carol. (1982). *In a different voice.* Cambridge: Harvard University Press.

Giroux, Henry A. (1981). *Ideology, culture and the process of schooling.* Philadelphia: Temple University Press.

Giroux, Henry A. (1983). Theories of reproduction and resistance in the new sociology of education: A critical analysis. *Harvard Educational Review, 53,* 257-93.

Glaspell, Susan. (1918). A jury of her peers. In Edward J. O'Brien (Ed.), *The best short stories of 1917.* London: Small, Maynard and Company.

Goswami, Dixie, & Stillman, Peter (Eds.). (1987). *Reclaiming the classroom: Teacher research as an agency for change.* Upper Montclair, NJ: Boyton/Cook.

Graff, Gerald. (1987). *Professing literature.* Chicago: University of Chicago Press.

Greenberg, Karen. (1984). Response to Farrell. *College Composition and Communication, 35,* 455-60.

Grice, H.P. (1975). Logic and conversation. In Peter Cole & Jerry L. Morgan (Eds.), *Syntax and semantics III: Speech acts.* New York: Academic Press.

Gumperz, John J. (1971). *Language in social groups.* Stanford: Stanford University Press.

Gumperz, John J. (1982). *Discourse strategies.* Cambridge: Cambridge University Press.

Gumperz, John J. (1986). Interactional sociolinguistics in the study of schooling. In Jenny Cook-Gumperz (Ed.), *The social construction of literacy.* Cambridge: Cambridge University Press.

Harding, Sandra, & Hintikka, Merrill B. (1983). *Discovering reality.* Boston: D. Reidel.

Hartwell, Patrick. (1984). Response to Farrell. *College Composition and Communication, 35,* 461–65.

Hawthorne, Nathaniel. (1974). The birth-mark. In *Mosses From an Old Manse.* Columbus: Ohio State University Press. (Original work published 1846)

Himley, Margaret. (1984). Response to Farrell. *College Composition and Communication, 35,* 465–68.

Healy, Mary K. (1987). Beating the "writing systems" on our own ground. *The Quarterly of the National Writing Project and the Center for the Study of Writing, 9* (1), 1–5.

Heath, Shirley Brice. (1982). Protean shapes in literacy events: ever shifting oral and literate traditions. In Deborah Tannen (Ed.), *Spoken and written language.* Norwood, NJ: Ablex.

Heath, Shirley Brice. (1983). *Ways with words.* Cambridge: Cambridge University Press.

Hemingway, Ernest. (1925). The Doctor and the doctor's wife. In *In Our Time.* New York: Charles Scribner's Sons.

Hoggart, Richard. (1957). *The uses of literacy.* New York: Oxford University Press.

Holland, Norman. (1975). *5 readers reading.* Cambridge: Yale University Press.

Holland, Norman. (1977). Transactive teaching: Cordelia's death. *College English, 39,* 276–285.

Holloway, Wendy. (1984). Gender differences in the production of subjectivity. In Julian Henriques (Eds.), *Changing the subject.* New York: Methuen.

Hurston, Zora Neale. (1978). *Their eyes were watching God.* Urbana: University of Illinois Press. (Original work published 1937)

Hymes, Dell. (1972). Models of the interactions of language and social life. In Dell Hymes & John J. Gumperz (Eds.), *Directions in sociolinguistics.* New York: Holt, Rinehart.

Iser, Wolfgang. (1978). *The act of reading.* Baltimore: Johns Hopkins University Press.

Kintgen, Eugene R. (1982). *The perception of poetry.* Bloomington: Indiana University Press.

Kozol, Jonathan. (1967). *Death at an early age.* New York: Bantam.

Kozol, Jonathan. (1985). *Illiterate America.* New York: Doubleday.

Labov, William. (1972). The logic of non-standard English. In *Language in the inner city*. Philadelphia: University of Pennsylvania Press.

Lincoln, Yvonne & Guba, Egon. (1985). *Naturalistic inquiry*. Beverly Hills: Sage Publications.

Lakoff, Robin. (1975). *Language and women's place*. New York: Harper and Row.

Lakoff, Robin Tolmach, & Scherr, Raquel. (1984). *Face-value: The politics of beauty*. London: Routledge and Kegan Paul.

Mailloux, Steven. (1982). *Interpretive conventions: The reader in American fiction*. Ithaca: Cornell University Press.

Melville, Herman. (1967). Benito Cereno. In Harold Beaver (Ed.), *Billy Budd, Sailor and other stories*. New York: Penguin. (Original work published 1856)

Myers, Greg. (1986). Reality, consensus, and reform in the rhetoric of composition teaching. *College English, 48*, 154–174.

Myers, Miles. (1987). Institutionalizing inquiry. *The Quarterly of the National Writing Project and the Center for the Study of Writing, 9*(3), 1–4.

Myers, Miles. (1985). *The teacher-researcher*. Urbana, IL: National Council of Teachers of English.

Nichols, Patricia. (1983). Linguistic options and choices for black women in the rural south. In Barrie Thorne, Cheris Kramarae, & Nancy Henley (Eds.), *Language, gender, and society*. Rowley, MA: Newbury.

Newkirk, Thomas. (Ed.). (1986). *Only connect*. Upper Montclair, NJ: Boyton/Cook.

Ogbu, John U. (1978). *Minority education and caste*. New York: Academic Press.

Ogbu, John U. (1987a). Opportunity structure, cultural boundaries, and literacy. In J. Langer (Ed.), *Language, literacy and culture*. Norwood, NJ: Ablex.

Ogbu, John U. (1987b). Variability in Minority School Performance: A Problem in Search of an Explanation. *Anthropology and Education Quarterly, 18*, 313–34.

Ohmann, Richard. (1976). *English in America*. New York: Oxford University Press.

Ohmann, Richard. (1982). Reflections on Class and Language. *College English, 44*, 1–17.

O'Neil, Wayne. (1971). The politics of bidialectalism. *College English, 33*, 433–38.

Ong, Walter. (1977). Literacy and orality in our times. *ADE Bulletin, 58*, 1–7.

Ong, Walter. (1982). *Orality and literacy*. London: Methuen.

Peterson, Bruce T. (Ed.). (1986). *Convergences*. Urbana, IL: National Council of Teachers of English.

Pratt, Mary Louise. (1977). *Toward a speech-act theory of literary discourse*. Bloomington: Indiana University Press.

Pratt, Mary Louise. (1986). Fieldwork in common places. In James Clifford & George E. Marcus (Eds.), *Writing culture*. Berkeley: University of California Press.

Richards, I.A. (1929). *Practical criticism*. New York: Harcourt.

Rorty, Richard. (1979). *Philosophy and the mirror of nature*. Princeton: Princeton University Press.

Rose, Mike. (1985). The language of exclusion. *College English, 47*, 341–59.

Rose, Mike. (1988). Narrowing the mind and the page. *College Composition and Communication, 39*, 267–302.

Rosen, Harold. (1985). The voices of communities and language in classrooms. *Harvard Educational Review, 55*, 448–56.

Rosenblatt, Louise. (1983). *Literature as exploration*. New York: Modern Language Association. (Original work published 1938)

Schutz, Alfred & Luckmann, Thoman. (1973). *The structures of the lifeworld*. (Richard M. Zaner and H. Tristram Engelhardt, Jr., Trans.). Evanston, IL: Northwestern University Press.

Scribner, Sylvia, & Cole, Michael. (1978). Literacy without schooling: Testing for intellectual effects. *Harvard Educational Review, 48*, 448–61.

Searle, John. (1969). *Speech acts: An essay in the philosophy of language*. New York: Cambridge University Press.

Sennett, Richard, & Cobb, Jonathan. (1973). *The hidden injuries of class*. New York: Viking.

Simon, Roger I., & Dippo, Donald. (1986). On critical ethnographic work. *Anthropology and Education Quarterly, 17*, 195–202.

Slatoff, Walter. (1970). *With respect to readers: Dimensions of literary response*. Ithaca, NY: Cornell University Press.

Sledd, James. (1969). Bi-dialectalism: the politics of white supremacy. *English Journal*, 1307–1329.

Sledd, James. (1984). In defense of *The Students' Right. College English, 46*, 667–75.

Smith, Dorothy E. (1979). A sociology for women. In Julia A. Sherman and Evelyn Torton Beck (Eds.), *The prism of sex: Essays in the sociology of knowledge*. Madison: University of Wisconsin Press.

Smitherman, Gevena. (1977). *Talkin and testifyin*. Boston: Houghton Mifflin.

Smitherman-Donalson, Gevena. (1988). Discriminatory Discourse on Afro-American Speech. In Geneva Smitherman-Donalson and Teun Van Dijk (Eds.), *Discourse and discrimination*. Detroit: Wayne State Press.

Spender, Dale. (1980). *Man made language*. London: Routledge and Kegan Paul.

Spender, Dale. (1981). Education: The patriarchal paradigm and the response to feminism. In Dale Spender (Ed.), *Men's studies modified.* Oxford: Pergamon Press.

Spender, Dale. (1982). *Invisible women: The schooling scandal.* London: Writers and Readers Press.

Stratton, R.E. (1984). Response to Farrell. *College Composition and Communication, 35,* 465–69.

Stubbs, Michael. (1983). *Language, schools and classrooms* (2nd ed.). New York: Methuen.

Students' Right to Their Own Language. (1974). *College Composition and Communication, 25.*

Suleiman, Susan. (Ed.). (1980). *The reader in the text.* Princeton, NJ: Princeton University Press.

Tannen, Deborah. (Ed.). (1982). *Spoken and written language.* Norwood, NJ: Ablex.

Thorne, Barrie, Kramarae, Cheris, & Henley, Nancy. (Eds.). (1983). *Language, gender, and society.* Rowley, MA: Newbury House.

Volosinov, V.N. (1973). *Marxism and the philosophy of language.* (L. Matejika & I.R. Titunk, Trans.). Cambridge: Harvard University Press.

Willis, Paul. (1977). *Learning to labor.* New York: Columbia University Press.

Woolf, Virginia. (1938). *Three guineas.* New York: Harcourt.

Author Index

A

Apple, M., 36, 37, *127*
Aronowitz, S., 35, 36, 37, 45, *127*
Austin, J.L., 15, *127*

B

Bartholomae, D., 3, 110, *127*
Beck, E.T., 47, *127*
Bereiter. C.. 91. *127*
Berlin, J., 111, *127*
Bernstein, B., 71, 72, 73, 74, 90, *127*
Berthoff, A.E., 35, 39, 111, *127*
Bissex, G., 35, *127*
Bizzell, P., 3, 4, 110, *127*
Bleich, D., 1, 2, 4, 5, 10, 12, 110, *127, 128*
Bourdieu, P., 20, *128*
Bowles, S., 20, *128*
Brannon, L., 39, 40, *128*
Brodkey, L., 30, *128*
Bruffee, K., 2, 3, 4, *128*
Bullock, R., 35, *127*

C

Cobb, J., 13, 84, 88, *132*
Cole, M., 95, 96, *132*
Cook-Gumperz, J., 93, *128*
Culler, J., 10, 12, *128*

D

Daeumer, E., 68, *128*
Davis, R.H., 40, 78, *128*
Derrida, J., 15, *128*
Deutsch. M. & Assoc.. 91. *128*
Dippo, D., 19, 35, *132*
Dittmar, N., 73, *128*

E

Elsasser, N., 38, *129*
Engelmann. S.. 91. *127*

F

Farrel, T., 92, 93, 96, 97, *129*
Fetterly, J., 10, 60, *129*
Fish, S., 3, 4, 10, 12, *129*
Flynn, E., 10, *129*
Freire, P., 25, 37, 38, 39, 43, *129*
Frye, M., 3, *129*

G

Garfinkel, H., 18, *129*
Geertz, C., 3, 19, 25, 34, 49, *129*
Gilligan. C.. 60. *129*
Gintis, H., *128*
Giroux, H.A., 20, 21, 22, 35, 36, 37, 45, 116, 117
Glaspell, S., 40, 58, 76, 82, *129*
Goswami, D., 35, *129*
Graff, G., 111, 119, *129*
Greenberg, K., 92, 93, *129*
Grice, H.P., 15, *129*
Guba, E., 50, 60, *131*
Gumperz, J.J., 17, 18, 93, 94, 98, 101, *128, 129, 130*

H

Harding, S., 3, *130*
Hartwell, P., 92, 93, *130*
Hawthorne, N., 53, *130*
Healy, M.K., 36, *130*
Heath, S.B., 25, 26, 30, 32, 33, 94, 95, 96, 98, *130*
Hemingway, E., 100, *130*
Henley, N., 59, *133*
Himley, M., 92, *130*
Hintikka, M.B., 3, *130*
Hoggart, R., 85, 86, 88, *130*
Holland, N., 10, 11, 12, 13, *130*
Holloway, W., 55, *130*
Hurston, Z.N., 58, 63, 65, *130*
Hymes, D., 26, *130*

I

Iser, W., 10, 12, *130*

J

John-Steiner, V.P., 38, *129*

K

Kintgen, E.R., 10, *130*
Knoblauch, C.H., 39, 40, *128*
Kozol, J., 29, 30, *130*
Kramarae, C., 59, *133*

L

Labov, W., 6, 26, 72, 91, 93, 94, 98, *131*
Lakoff, R.T., 55, 59, 60, *131*
Lincoln, Y., 50, *131*
Luckmann, T., 42, *132*

M

Mailloux, S., 10, 13, *131*
Melville, H., 76, 82, *131*
Myers, G., 4, *131*
Myers, M., 35, *131*

N

Newkirk, T., 118, *131*
Nichols, P., 52, *131*

O

Ogbu, J.U., 13, 33, 34, 35, 117, *131*
Ohmann, R., 9, 12, 13, 43, 44, 72, 73, 74, 81, 117, *131*
O'Neil, W., 97, *131*
Ong, W., 91, 92, 93, 94, 96, *131*

P

Passeron, J.P., 20, *128*
Peterson, B.T., 118, *132*

Petrosky, A., 110, *127*
Pratt, M.L., 30, 93, 94, *132*

R

Richards, I.A., *132*
Rorty, R., 3, 4, *132*
Rose, M., 109, 111, *132*
Rosen, H., 32, *132*
Rosenblatt, L., *132*

S

Scherr, R., 55, 59, 60, *131*
Schutz, A., 42, *132*
Scribner, S., 95, 96, *132*
Searle, J., 15, *132*
Sennett, R., 13, 84, 88, *132*
Shaughnessy, M., 110
Simon, R.I., 19, 35, 85, *132*
Slatoff, W., 10, *132*
Sledd, J., 97, 129, *132*
Smith, D.E., 57, *132*
Smitherman-Donalson, G., 93, 96, 98, 107, *132*
Spender, D., 3, 13, 51, 59, 111, 113, 117, *132, 133*
Stillman, P., 35, *129*
Stratton, R.E., 92, *133*
Stubbs, M., 73, *133*
Suleiman, S., 12, *133*

T

Tannen, D., 94, 95, 96, *133*
Thorne, B., 59, *133*

V

Volosinov, V.N., *133*

W

Willis, P., 21, 117, *133*
Woolf, V., 111, *133*

Subject Index

A
Academic discourse, 4, 16, 117
Activist teaching, 43–45, 49
Agency, 15, 20
Analysis (as an intellectual ability), 92, 93n, 94
Audience, 52, 55–56, 68–69, 79, 86, 98, 101
Authoritarian teaching, 43–44
Authority
  in Mr. H's writing, 61, 65–66, 67–68, 70
  of the Teacher, 43, 87

B
Bidialectalism, 97, 97n, 98
Beauty, 53–55, 56, 59–60
Black English, 6, 31, 90, 93, 97–98, 102, 105, 106–107
Black students, 89, 90, 92, 97–98

C
Case study research, 49–50
Civil Rights, 6
Class, 1–2, 6, 11, 14, 16, 18, 20, 22, 35, 38, 49, 71–88, 101, 109, 115, 117
Code-switching, 101, 102–104
Cognitive ability, 84–86, 92–93, 94, 95–97, 106, 115
Competition, 61–64, 69–70
Compliance with the teacher, 6, 39, 45, 69, 87, 105
Constraints (in interpretation), 18
Conversation, 2, 94, 96, 101, 116
Context (in interpreting language), 15–19, 51–52, 59, 71, 72, 73–75, 91, 94, 96, 116
Critical ethnography, 19–20, 30, 35

D
Deficit theories, 21, 72, 73n, 90–94, 93n, 96, 102, 107
Deskilling, 36, 111

Double-context, 1, 18, 71, 83, 90, 98

E
Elaborated codes, 71, 72, 73, 88
Ethnography, 18–20, 25–36, 49
Evaluation, 39, 42, 45, 46, 110, 116

F
Feminism, 3, 6, 13, 111–114
Feminist Criticism Group (Indiana University), 1

G
Gender, 1–2, 5, 12, 13, 14, 16, 18, 20, 22, 23, 35, 38, 49, 50, 51–70, 71, 109, 111–114, 115, 117
Generic Writing Systems, 36–37
Grading, 45–46, 80, 81, 84, 99

H
Hierarchies, 32, 52, 116
  in Mr. H's writing, 64, 65–66, 69, 70
History
  disciplinary, 14, 19, 110–111
  educational, 14, 25, 42, 43, 107, 110
  in *Ways With Words* (Heath), 31, 34
  minority cultures', 33–34
  Ms. N's in English classes, 98–100, 107
  of the classroom, 1, 36, 38, 42, 43
  students', 9, 16, 23, 38, 42, 43, 47
Hypothetical readers, 12, 13

I
Identity theme (Holland), 10, 11
Individualism, 3, 7, 9, 10, 12, 13, 15, 19, 20, 47
  in Mr. C's writing, 76, 78–79, 81, 84, 85, 86–88
  in Mr. H's writing, 70
Intelligence testing, 85

Interactive pedagogy, 13–21, 22–23, 25, 27, 49, 50, 117, 120
Interpretation, 11, 12–13, 19, 23
  in writing courses, 109–111, 115–116
  of classrooms, 109–111, 115–116
  of ethnography, 30, 31, 34
  of language, 6, 17
  of literature, 56, 57, 58, 60, 64–66, 109
  of social background, 18, 21–22
  of students, 22–23, 110n, 115–116

J
Judgment, 114–116
  in Mr. C's writing, 76–77, 82, 84–85, 87

L
Line of fault (Smith), 57, 60

M
Marxism, 3, 6, 11
Masculine ideology, 7, 67
Masculinity and writing, 59–68
Minority students, 1, 6, 7, 21, 22, 118, 120
Motivational explanation, 54, 55

N
Natural narratives, 93–94
New Criticism, 43–44

O
Oppositional culture, 33, 117–118, 118–119
Orality and literacy, 91–96, 93n, 98

P
Paper commenting, 39–42
Persuasion, 51, 61, 65, 68, 69–70
Politics of teaching, 3–5, 6–7, 20–22, 34, 35, 35–38, 43–47, 107, 112–113
Problem-posing (Freire), 37–43, 45–46, 114
Profanity (in Mr. H's writing), 68
Protective strategies, 57–59

R
Race, 1–2, 5, 14, 16, 18, 19–20, 22, 35, 38, 49, 50, 89–107, 109, 115, 117
Racism, 29, 31, 32, 98, 118
Reader-response criticism, 1, 10, 10n, 12, 12n, 60n
Reflective explanation, 54, 64
Reproduction, 20
Resistance, 20–22, 109, 115–116, 117
Restricted codes, 71–72, 74

S
Scholarship boy (Hoggart), 85–86
Service courses, 118–119
Speech act theory, 15, 16
Social approaches to writing, 2–5
Social construction, 2–4, 4n, 55, 113, 114
Social identity, 7, 8, 10–11, 14, 15
Standard English, 89, 90, 97–98, 99, 102, 103, 104, 105
Standardized tests, 29, 95
Stereotypes, 49, 51, 56, 71–72, 76, 82
Student (ideology of), 7, 9–10, 19
Stylistic explanation of language variation, 33, 72–73

T
Teacher-researcher, 35
Textbooks, 9–10, 12, 13
Transformative intellectual (Giroux and Aronowitz), 35, 37
Typification, 42–43, 45–46

U
Upward mobility, 82, 84–85, 85–86

W
Women's language, 49, 51–52, 59
Women students, 1, 6, 7, 21, 22, 89, 90, 118, 120
Working-class language, 71–75, 81n, 82–83
Working-class students, 1, 6, 7, 18, 21, 22, 89, 90, 118, 120